EXTREME DINOSAURS

To Sophia

Love - & Chow-Chow

HarperCollins books may be purchased for educational, business, or sales promotional use. For information, please write: Special Markets Department, HarperCollins Publishers, 10 East 53rd Street, New York, NY 10022.

Produced for HarperCollins by:

HYDRA PUBLISHING
129 MAIN STREET
IRVINGTON, NY 10533
WWW.HYLASPUBLISHING.COM

FIRST EDITION

The name of the "Smithsonian," "Smithsonian Institution," and the sunburst logo are registered trademarks of the Smithsonian Institution.

Library of Congress Cataloging-in-Publication Data

Parker, Steve.
  Extreme dinosaurs / Steve Parker and Leslie Mertz.—1st ed.
    p. cm.
  Includes index.
  ISBN 978-0-06-089142-8
  1. Dinosaurs. I. Mertz, Leslie A. II. Title.

QE861.4.P365 2008
567.9—dc22

2007034384

08 09 10 11   QW   10 9 8 7 6 5 4 3 2 1

EXTREME DINOSAURS

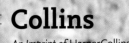

Collins

An Imprint of HarperCollinsPublishers

Steve Parker and Leslie Mertz

Contents

Green River Canyon in Dinosaur National Monument

Monsters of the Mesozoic

How can people get so excited about animals which they have never seen in the flesh? How can we be thrilled by creatures which we can never experience in real life, because they lived so long ago? Why are some people not just enthusiastic about these beasts, but awestruck and occasionally even terrified?

Dinosaurs manage to captivate us from well beyond the grave. In fact their "graves" are the key, since they hold preserved remains such as bones, teeth, claws, horns and other tough parts of their once-living bodies. These fossils are clues to the existence of dinosaurs long ago, and the evidence is rock-solid.

Extreme Examples

Well-known dinosaurs such as terrible *Tyrannosaurus*, huge *Brachiosaurus*, and horned *Triceratops* were among the most impressive beasts ever to walk the Earth. The dinosaur group brims with extreme examples of big-toothed carnivores, massive herbivores, and small, dainty omnivores.

Part of the dinosaurs' allure is that we must study and imagine many of their kind while peering back into the mists of time. Dinosaurs lived through most of the Mesozoic Era, which dated from about 251 to 65 million years ago. Evidence for the earliest dinosaurs goes back to around 230 million years. "Mesozoic" means "Middle Life," but in popular terminology, the Mesozoic can also be called the "Age of Dinosaurs." In contrast, beasts like woolly mammoths and sabertooth cats, and our own apelike ancestors, date back just a few million years.

Scientific Advances

Recent decades have seen a revolution in views on dinosaurs. They did not all die out 65 million years ago, in the infamous end-of-Cretaceous mass extinction. This knowledge stems from the way that scientists work out the evolutionary relationships of organisms. The dinosaur group, known as a clade, encompasses all creatures that evolved from an original common ancestor—popularly, the "first dinosaur." It is now established that birds evolved from dinosaurs. So, in modern terminology, birds are dinosaurs, and therefore the dinosaur group still flourishes today, in the form of birds.

This approach has come from enormous changes in the way that extinct dinosaurs from the Mesozoic are analyzed and reconstructed. Paleontologists use the scientific methods of formulating and testing hypotheses, generating theories that are subject to constant testing, and revising knowledge from the resulting

A hungry *Ceratosaurus* surprises a *Brachiosaurus* in the Late Jurassic. While we surmise that dinosaurs killed and ate each other, little is known about the specifics of their interactions.

Tracks dated to the Cretaceous on Dinosaur Ridge in Colorado are all that remain of a herd of iguanodontid dinosaurs. Footprints like these provide clues to behavior and habitat.

Reconstructing Dinosaurs

Techniques such as comparative anatomy and phylogenetic inference, allied to the knowledge that birds are dinosaurs, allows science-based predictions for extinct Mesozoic dinosaurs. These include proposals on how they fed and moved, their predatory behavior, body chemistry (metabolism), and intelligence. The ways that some of those Mesozoic dinosaurs may have raised their young can be inferred, based on the similarities in nest structure, and on hatchling bone anatomy, between extinct dinosaurs and modern birds.

Also, fossils themselves provide evidence for not only anatomy, but also for functions and processes. Preserved remains such as footprints and tail drags are viewed as "frozen behavior."

evidence. Two important techniques are comparative anatomy and phylogenetic inference. Comparative anatomy uses accumulated knowledge of animal structures, and their associated biologies, to make comparisons and contrasts. Phylogenetic inference involves reconstructing missing data based on evolutionary relationships. Put simply, closely related individuals tend to share a larger number of similar features than do distantly related individuals, as a result of their shared common ancestry. If two kinds of animals, one living and one extinct, have a close evolutionary relationship, then certain similarities between them can be inferred, and these inferences tested scientifically.

Magnolias were one of the earliest flowering plants to appear. Still flourishing today, such plants first appeared in the Cretaceous Period.

Combining all these methods helps the understanding of dinosaurs' actions, activities, and lifestyles, whether they were clever or dull-witted, and how they might have acted in their daily lives and breeding years.

Rulers of the Earth

As far as we know from fossils, Mesozoic dinosaurs ruled the land. Few other groups of creatures have dominated terrestrial habitats as they did. Their fossils have been found on every continent—although the global map was very different then, due to the ongoing process of plate tectonics and what is sometimes called "continental drift." In some locations, fossil dinosaur bones number thousands upon thousands, suggesting enormous groups that met a sudden common fate.

Dinosaurs were far from alone in their Mesozoic habitats. They lived, as animals now, as part of a complex web of life. Fossils show a huge variety of creatures sharing their landscapes. These included an extensive range of reptiles, many of which are now extinct; various mammals, from small and shrewlike up to badger-sized; and an immense range of invertebrates (animals without backbones), such as worms and grubs, cockroaches and dragonflies and other insects, scorpions, millipedes, and myriad others.

Hosts of plants, some familiar from today, but others long extinct, were prominent. They formed the basis of food chains and energy transfers among Mesozoic animals. To understand the dinosaurs, and how they fed, bred, survived and died, requires an appreciation of how they fitted into their Mesozoic ecosystems.

Continuing Change

Avian dinosaurs, in the form of birds, are still with us. Mesozoic dinosaurs are long gone, and how they lived and died can never change. But our views on them can. New fossil discoveries capture headlines and overturn established theories. Scientists advance methods of locating and analyzing fossil remains, and extend the accumulated knowledge of organisms that populated Mesozoic habitats. Traditional views are challenged, and records are rewritten. Views on dinosaurs are endlessly gripping and, like life itself, continually evolving.

Dinosaurs shared the Earth with a host of other creatures, such as this *Pteranodon* from the Cretaceous Period.

What Was a Dinosaur?

The term *dinosaur* conjures up different images for different people. To some, almost any extinct beast with big teeth fits the bill. To others, dinosaurs are limited to a few famous characters such as *Tyrannosaurus*, *Diplodocus*, *Iguanodon*, and *Stegosaurus*, and little else.

Vertebrates

As members of the animal kingdom, dinosaurs are placed in the great group known as the vertebrates. This encompasses creatures with an internal skeleton which incorporates a row of vertebrae, commonly known as backbones, forming the spinal column. Familiar living vertebrates are fish, amphibians such as frogs and salamanders, reptiles, birds, and mammals from mice to whales, including ourselves.

Within the vertebrates, the characteristics of the typical dinosaur skeleton place it in the traditional group known as Reptilia. The features include the layout and joints in the jaws and skull, and also certain elements of the vertebrae and limb bones. Scaly skin is another indicative (but not exclusive) reptilian feature, and samples of fossilized skin scales are associated with dinosaur remains.

Archosaurs

Among the reptiles, dinosaurs belong to a group known as the archosaurs or "ruling reptiles." These can be distinguished by several skeletal features,

A small *Iguanodon* herd traverses the Early Cretaceous landscape. Based on fossil evidence and comparisons to living creatures, scientists believe that these and some other herbivorous dinosaurs traveled in groups.

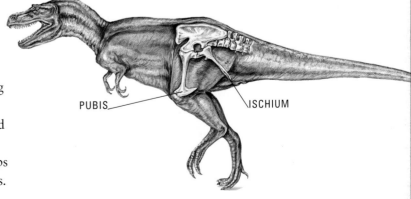

ISCHIUM

PUBIS

such as "windows" in the
skull in front of the eye
sockets (orbits), known
as antorbital fenestrae,
and a particular shape to the calcaneus
ankle bone. The archosaurs encompass dinosaurs (nonavian and avian),
the winged reptilelike fliers known as
pterosaurs, crocodiles and alligators,
and certain other long extinct groups.

Distinguishing a Dinosaur

Further skeletal features mark out
dinosaurs from other archosaurs. For
example, a hole or "window" in the
socket area (acetabulum) of the hip
bone, or pelvis, is a typical dinosaur
characteristic. Another is a prominent
up-pointing projection, or ascend-
ing process, on the astragalus (upper
ankle bone). Overall there is a "suite"
of 10–15 characteristics, all discern-
ible from fossils, which can be used to
diagnose a dinosaur.

More simply, perhaps, and as
seen in birds today, most dinosaurs had legs which were relatively
straight and positioned below the
body, rather than bent and sprawling
to the sides as in crocodiles, turtles,
and lizards. This upright posture and
erect gait allowed efficient, energy-
saving movement, which was perhaps
one reason for the dinosaurs' success.

The Importance of Hips

Within the dinosaur group are
two great subgroups based on
hip structure. In the saurischian or "lizard-hipped" dinosaurs,
the pubis bone projects at an angle
down and forward, while the ischium
projects down but slopes rearward.
In the ornithischian or "bird-hipped"
dinosaurs the pubis lies roughly parallel to the ischium, with both elements
directed down and back.

Briefly, saurischians include all
meat-eating or predatory dinosaurs,
from tiny *Compsognathus* to medium-
sized *Deinonychus* and giants like
Tyrannosaurus, and also the large, long-
necked, herbivorous sauropods such as
Diplodocus. Ornithischians were plant-
eaters and range from well-known
Iguanodon and dainty *Hypsilophodon*
to *Stegosaurus*, horned *Triceratops*, and
armored *Ankylosaurus*.

In ornithischians like
Edmontosaurus (above),
the pubis and ischium
are parallel, while in
saurischians such as
Albertosaurus (below),
the pubis points forwards.

PUBIS

ISCHIUM

Dinosaur Timeline

The history of large, multi-cellular life on Earth covers three great spans of time known as the Paleozoic, Mesozoic, and Cenozoic Eras. Dinosaurs flourished for most of the middle span, the Mesozoic (251–65 million years ago). This era is divided into three major time segments called periods, which are named as follows:

- Triassic Period
  (251–200 million years ago)
- Jurassic Period
  (200–145 million years ago)
- Cretaceous Period
  (145–65 million years ago)

Like all organisms, dinosaurs were products of their time. They evolved to suit contemporary environmental conditions such as the climate, vegetation, and landscape, and also other animals around them, which could be prey, predators, or competitors for resources such as living space.

Summary of the "Age of Dinosaurs"

The earliest evidence for dinosaurs dates from almost 230 million years ago, during the Early Late Triassic Period, especially in what is now Argentina, South America. The dinosaur group rapidly spread and diversified, with many new kinds evolving on almost all continents by the end of the Triassic.

During the Jurassic Period more new groups appeared, and toward the end of this time some true giants strode across the land, such as the carnivore *Allosaurus* and the sauropod *Brachiosaurus*.

By the Early Cretaceous Period, more new groups were evolving, including even larger and more diverse plant-eaters and new forms of predators.

As the Cretaceous Period continued, more unusual body forms developed, such as the hadrosaurs or duckbilled dinosaurs, the ceratopsians or horned dinosaurs, the pachycephalosaurs or "boneheads," and the ornithomimosaurs or ostrich dinosaurs. But the dinosaurs' reign was brought to an abrupt end by the mass extinction at the end of the Cretaceous Period, 65 million years ago; only avian dinosaurs survived.

Below: Satellite image showing present-day Earth.

Opposite: Images showing how Earth may have looked 240 million years ago (top), 170 million years ago (middle), and 90 million years ago (bottom).

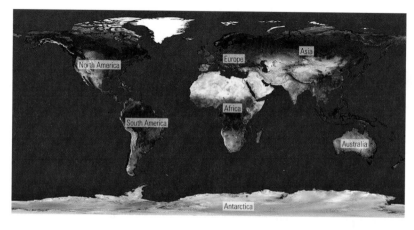

North America
Europe
Asia
Africa
South America
Australia
Antarctica

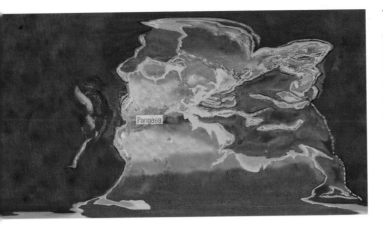

Triassic Period

All continents were together as one vast land mass, Pangaea. Its northern part comprised North America, Europe, and most of Asia. The southern portion consisted of South America, Africa, Arabia, India, Antarctica, and Australia. Toward the end of the period, Pangaea began to crack apart.

Globally the climate was mild to hot, but relatively dry. Around the edges of Pangaea some regions were moist, but sparsely vegetated deserts occupied much of the interior. Dominant trees were mostly conifers along with ginkgos. Cycads, some tall and palmlike and others short and squat, and seed ferns flourished, while ferns carpeted the ground.

Jurassic Period

Pangaea continued to break up as northern Laurasia fragmented away from southern Gondwana. The early Atlantic Ocean opened between North America and Europe, and then, much later, between South America and Africa. Later, India prepared for its long drift northward.

Warmth and moisture dominated this period, with limited seasonal variation. Forests included types of pines and sequoias, along with ginkgos, cycadeoids, and seed ferns, with ground cover of ferns and horsetails.

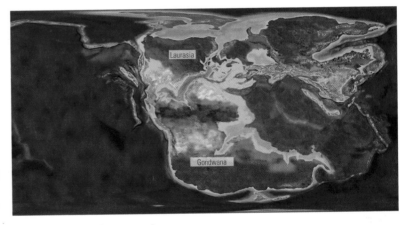

Cretaceous Period

Laurasia was overridden by shallow seas, so that western and eastern North America were separated. Eastern North America, Greenland, and Europe were also separate land masses. Gondwana fragmented as its continents all began to move toward their present positions.

Conifers and other Jurassic trees still cloaked the land at first. By the middle of the period, early angiosperms, or flowering plants (flowers, herbs, and broadleaf trees), dotted the landscape. They spread and diversified, as various types of magnolias, maples, oaks, and walnuts flourished, along with the first grasses.

Main Dinosaur Groups

SUMMARY OF THE MAIN DINOSAUR GROUPS

<table>
<tr><td rowspan="13">SAURISCHIANS</td><td>THEROPODS</td><td>"Beast feet"</td><td>Walked exclusively on their hind limbs. Almost all were carnivorous, exclusively or to a great extent.</td><td></td></tr>
<tr><td>Coelophysoids</td><td>"Hollow forms"</td><td>Predatory dinosaurs known from the Late Triassic to the beginning of the Jurassic. Typically, they were slender, long-necked, and mid-sized.</td><td>*Coelophysis, Dilophosaurus*</td></tr>
<tr><td>Ceratosaurs</td><td>"Horn lizards"</td><td>Early predatory dinosaurs. They were displaced in northern continents by other meat-eaters, but persisted in southern lands almost to the end of the Cretaceous.</td><td>*Ceratosaurus, Carnotaurus*</td></tr>
<tr><td>Spinosaurs</td><td>"Spine lizards"</td><td>Large to huge long-jawed hunters from Europe, Africa, and South America, mainly during the Early Cretaceous.</td><td>*Spinosaurus, Baryonyx, Suchomimus*</td></tr>
<tr><td>Allosaurs</td><td>"Other lizards"</td><td>Mostly big to huge, enormous-fanged meat-eaters, mainly from the Late Jurassic in North and South America, Europe, and Africa.</td><td>*Allosaurus, Giganotosaurus, Carcharodontosaurus*</td></tr>
<tr><td>Tyrannosaurs</td><td>"Tyrant lizards"</td><td>Among the largest and most fearsome of the predatory dinosaurs, mainly from North America and Asia during the Cretaceous, especially toward its end.</td><td>*Tyrannosaurus, Albertosaurus, Alioramus*</td></tr>
<tr><td>Ornithomimosaurs</td><td>"Bird-mimic lizards"</td><td>Long, slim neck, tail, and limbs, and a toothless beak-shaped mouth characterized these Late Cretaceous fast runners, from North America, Asia, and elsewhere.</td><td>*Gallimimus, Ornithomimus, Struthiomimus*</td></tr>
<tr><td>Oviraptors</td><td>"Egg stealers"</td><td>Smallish and slender, with a deep, parrotlike beaked mouth, mainly from Late Cretaceous Asia.</td><td>*Oviraptor, Ingenia, Conchoraptor*</td></tr>
<tr><td>Dromaeosaurs</td><td>"Running lizards"</td><td>Small to medium, fast-moving hunters of the Early to Late Cretaceous, especially from northern continents. Often known as "raptors."</td><td>*Deinonychus, Utahraptor, Velociraptor, Dromaeosaurus*</td></tr>
<tr><td>SAUROPODOMORPHS</td><td>"Lizard feet forms"</td><td>Mostly medium to huge, walking on all fours. Typically long-necked and long-tailed, barrel-shaped body, four columnlike limbs.</td><td></td></tr>
<tr><td>Prosauropods</td><td>"Before lizard-feet"</td><td>Early forms of the bulky, long-necked, long-tailed plant-eaters, especially from Europe and South America.</td><td>*Plateosaurus, Riojasaurus, Sellosaurus*</td></tr>
<tr><td>Cetiosaurs and early sauropods</td><td>"Whale lizards"</td><td>Varied medium to large sauropods from the Early to Middle Jurassic, probably an assemblage of various evolutionary lines.</td><td>*Cetiosaurus, Shunosaurus, Vulcanodon*</td></tr>
<tr><td>Diplodocids</td><td>"Double beams"</td><td>Large to very large plant-eaters, usually with front limbs shorter than the rear ones, mainly from Late Jurassic North America.</td><td>*Diplodocus, Barosaurus, Apatosaurus*</td></tr>
</table>

Background: Model of
Triceratops

	Group	Meaning	Description	Examples
	Brachiosaurs	"Arm lizards"	Among the most massive of all dinosaurs, with elongated front limbs for a giraffelike profile, mainly from North America, Europe, and Africa.	*Brachiosaurus, Sauroposeidon*
	Titanosaurs	"Titanic lizards"	Big to enormous sauropods, mainly from the Cretaceous Period of South America but with representatives on almost all continents.	*Saltasaurus, Argentinosaurus*
ORNITHISCHIANS	THYREOPHORANS	"Shield bearers"	Herbivorous, quadrupedal, armored dinosaurs. Known throughout the Jurassic and the Cretaceous Periods.	
	Scelidosaurs and others	"Lower leg lizards"	Early, smallish, partly armored plant-eaters, varied in shape and probably in origins, with representatives mainly from the northern continents during the Jurassic.	*Scelidosaurus, Scutellosaurus, Emausaurus*
	Stegosaurs	"Roofed lizards"	Hump-backed herbivores with a low-slung head and tail, and large upright plates or spikes along the back, mainly from Jurassic times in the northern continents and Africa.	*Stegosaurus, Kentrosaurus, Tuojiangosaurus*
	Ankylosaurs	"Fused lizards"	Heavily armored, low-bodied plant-eaters that appeared in the Jurassic and spread widely during the Cretaceous.	*Ankylosaurus, Euoplocephalus, Edmontonia, Nodosaurus*
	MARGINOCEPHALIANS	"Margin headed lizards"	Characterized by bony structures at the top or rear of the skull. Exclusively herbivorous, but both bipedal and quadrupedal species are known.	
	Pachycephalosaurs	"Thick headed lizards"	Small to medium herbivores with large rear limbs, characterized by a thickened dome of bone at the top of the skull. Chiefly from Cretaceous North America and Asia.	*Stegoceras, Prenocephale, Pachycephalosaurus*
	Ceratopsians	"Horned-faces,"	Bulky Cretaceous herbivores developing varied designs of facial horns and neck frills.	*Triceratops, Styracosaurus, Centrosaurus*
	ORNITHOPODS	"Bird feet"	Three-toed (early species retained four) herbivores, largely semi-quadrupedal. Very common in the Cretaceous Period.	
	Heterodontosaurs and early ornithopods	"Different tooth lizards"	Small, early plant-eaters from various regions, running fast on long rear limbs, mostly from the Jurassic but persisting into the Cretaceous.	*Heterodontosaurus, Hypsilophodon, Thescelosaurus*
	Iguanodontians	"Iguana teeth"	Medium-sized to larger herbivores with a two- or four-legged gait, widespread and common especially during the Cretaceous Period.	*Iguanodon, Altirhinus, Ouranosaurus*
	Hadrosaurs	"Bulky lizards"	Large herbivores moving mainly on their rear limbs, with a toothless, ducklike beak at the front of the mouth and batteries of chewing teeth behind. Chiefly Cretaceous, known from many continents.	*Corythosaurus, Maiasaura, Saurolophus, Lambeosaurus*

Dinosaur Fossil Hot Spots

For more than 160 years, the discovery of dinosaur fossils has spread and shifted around the world. Many promising new sites are probed annually. But the spotlight only shines on a select few, which yield significant remains and rise to the status of "dinosaur hot spot." Some of these sites are turned into national parks, and some have made the grade of World Heritage Sites.

The term "dinosaur" began in 1841–42. As chronicled later in this book, English comparative anatomist Richard Owen coined the name Dinosauria for a group of fossil reptiles with distinctive features. During the mid-nineteenth century various sites in Europe (1) were the first hot spots for dinosaur fossils. One of the most famous is Bernissart, Belgium (2), where more than 30 almost complete *Iguanodon* skeletons were discovered deep in a coal mine in 1878.

West and East

North America was not far behind Europe and saw its first wave of "dinosaur fever" from the 1860s. Towards the end of the century the "badlands" of the American western interior (3) were a major hot spot, as teams led by rivals Othniel Charles Marsh and Edward Drinker Cope vied to discover and name the most dinosaurs and other extinct vertebrates. Canada's Red Deer River, Alberta (4), was also a focus location as the nineteenth century closed and the twentieth unfolded.

In the 1920s U.S.-led expeditions to the Gobi Desert (5) uncovered tremendous new finds of Late Cretaceous dinosaurs, their nests, and eggs. More exciting revelations came in China (6) from the 1930s, with another wave of discoveries there from the 1970s.

Going South

Mesozoic dinosaur remains had been found in all southern continents except Antarctica by the early 1900s. From the 1930s in South America finds increased pace, especially in Argentina (7), which hit the headlines with many record-breaking new fossils from the 1980s and 1990s. These included an early dinosaur *Herrerasaurus*, the huge predator *Giganotosaurus*, and the vast sauropod *Argentinosaurus*.

Australia's "Dinosaur Cove" near Melbourne (8) has yielded many important remains and stimulated numerous ideas about how dinosaurs may have survived seasonally cold climates. Antarctica was the last continent to yield dinosaur remains, from 1986.

In the past few years, the spotlight has again swung east and south. Some of the most astonishing discoveries have come from China, especially the Liaoning region, where increasing numbers of exquisitely preserved dinosaurs show a variety of feather-like coverings. Argentina continues to yield impressive fossils, and both West Africa (9) and the island nation of Madagascar (10) have hit the headlines for the discoveries being made there.

DINOSAUR RECORD HOLDERS

CHAPTER 1

BIGGEST
MEAT-EATERS

RECORDS, EXTREMES, AND SUPREMES endlessly intrigue. Biggest is especially fascinating—particularly when it is a huge meat-eating predator, mouth filled with deadly fangs, and a gape that could easily accommodate a human being. No wonder *Tyrannosaurus* is one of the world's best-known creatures, even though it perished 65 million years ago. Formerly famed as the biggest meat-eater in history, *Tyrannosaurus* has been challenged in recent years by a rash of newly discovered fossils which reveal even greater hunters.

When reconstructing dinosaurs, especially if they are potential record breakers, caution is key. This applies particularly to specimens where only small fragments remain—which, in paleontology, is the vast majority of cases. People naturally wish to focus on the extremes of estimates, rather than the more considered middle range of measurements. The following pages include several claimants to the throne of largest-ever land meat-eater. In some cases, there is a lack of fossil material for full assessment, and it is with caution that they should be hailed as newly crowned champions.

Left: One of the best-known dinosaurs, *Tyrannosaurus rex* ("tyrant lizard king") may have been a scavenger as well as active hunter. First described in 1905, *Tyrannosaurus* maintains its status in popular imagination, even though it now has several competitors for the title of largest carnivorous dinosaur. Pages 12–13: *Archaeopteryx* was one of the first links between dinosaurs and modern birds ever to be discovered.

First with a Name

In 1824 Oxford scholar William Buckland (1784–1856) became president of the prestigious Geological Society of London. That same year he published an account of fossils discovered several years earlier in Stonesfield Quarry, near Oxford, England. He described several fossils as belonging to some form of large, long-gone reptile. Buckland named the beast *Megalosaurus*, "great lizard." This was the first scientific name bestowed on a dinosaur. However, Buckland knew nothing of this, since the term *dinosaur* would not be coined for another 18 years.

Scant Remains

The fossils examined by Buckland included a length of lower jaw with teeth, some vertebrae (backbones), and assorted portions of a scapula (shoulder blade), pelvis (hip bone), and hind limb bones. The jaw was especially striking, with one long, sharp, fully grown mature tooth, and several shorter, younger, part-grown teeth.

These fossils were quite probably not from one individual, but two or more. They had already been examined by Georges Cuvier (1769–1832), the enormously influential French comparative anatomist and one of

This illustration, 1859, of *Megalosaurus* by Samuel Goodrich shows a more lizardlike dinosaur than modern conceptions. In particular, scientists believe *Megalosaurus* to have been bipedal.

Europe's most respected scientists. On a visit to Buckland, Cuvier agreed that the remains represented a lizardlike reptile of some kind. At different times, Buckland variously estimated the length of *Megalosaurus* at 23 to 40 feet (7–12 m).

A Wastebasket Genus

Over the following decades, any fossils that remotely resembled a large meat-eating reptile were casually named *Megalosaurus*. The supposed geographic range of the "great lizard" spread as remains fitting its description were reported from France, Belgium, and Germany, then Portugal, and farther-flung regions. Eventually, alleged *Megalosaurus* fossils were being dug up in North America and even Australia. Thus the name *Megalosaurus* became a "wastebasket genus" for all these various fossils. To add to the confusion, early reconstructions showed *Megalosaurus* resembling a stiff-legged crocodile, with a low, midline, sail-like crest of skin between its shoulders—due to vertebrae from a different dinosaur, the spinosaur *Altispinax*, being drafted in as substitutes for missing *Megalosaurus* backbones.

Modern Views

In recent times, many of the so-called *Megalosaurus* specimens have been

A SCIENTIFIC ECCENTRIC

William Buckland, namer of *Megalosaurus*, was not only an accomplished geologist, but also a dedicated churchman, appointed canon of Christ's College, Oxford, in 1825. Less conventionally, he was an enthusiastic diner who claimed to have eaten his way through most of the animal kingdom. His dishes included mouse, big cats, and crocodiles, although he announced that he was less fond of bluebottle flies and mole meat.

restudied and assigned to other genera. For example, in 1964 one of the better-preserved English specimens was renamed *Eustreptospondylus*, and some of the North American remains are now regarded as *Dilophosaurus*.

Megalosaurus remains a generally poorly known, medium-large carnivore from Late Jurassic times in Europe. It was perhaps a cousin of North America's *Allosaurus*. At first glance its reconstruction might resemble *Allosaurus* or *Tyrannosaurus* in overall body form and posture. *Megalosaurus* was probably around 30 feet (9 m) in length and 1 ton in weight. Various trackways, or series of fossilized footprints, have been attributed to it, including some fine sets near Ardley, England, uncovered in 1997. These may show its progress across what is now the rolling Oxfordshire countryside.

Terror of the Late Jurassic

One of the larger meat-eating dinosaurs, and certainly among the largest land carnivores of the Jurassic Period, was North America's *Allosaurus* ("other/strange lizard"). At more than 30 feet (9 m) long, and weighing in at perhaps 2 tons, it would have been a great threat even to large sauropods of its time and place, such as *Diplodocus* and *Apatosaurus*.

Confusing Origins

Like many dinosaurs first unearthed in the late nineteenth century, *Allosaurus* suffered confusions during its naming and identification. Its various remains were called *Poicilopleuron* and *Antrodemus*, among other designations. In 1883, a particularly fine series of partial skeletons, and one much more complete specimen, were uncovered in the Garden Park Quarry, Fremont County, Colorado. These specimens were carefully prepared at the Smithsonian Institution by Charles Gilmore (1874–1945),

The skull of *Allosaurus* sported several fenestrae, or windows, making the head lighter.

who in 1920 identified them as *Antrodemus*. However, later studies showed that they had far more in common with an earlier (1877) find at the same quarry, which Othniel Charles Marsh had titled *Allosaurus*.

Mass Graveyard

Phases of excavations at what is now the world famous Cleveland-Lloyd Dinosaur Quarry, Utah, began in 1927, by the University of Utah. Further discoveries came in 1939 by a team from Princeton University, and then Utah again in 1960. The results include thousands of bones representing, among other dinosaurs such as *Stegosaurus* and *Camptosaurus*, probably more than 60 *Allosaurus*. These include individuals at various life or growth stages.

It is tempting to suggest that *Allosaurus* roamed in mixed-age herds and perhaps even hunted in packs. But most of the specimens are disarticulated, that is, their bones have come apart and were scattered, rather than being articulated, or positioned as though jointed in life. Perhaps various large herbivores such as *Stegosaurus* became trapped in soft ground, such as a marsh. Lone *Allosaurus* individuals may have been attracted and gathered around the strugglers, but they too were sucked to their doom.

Designed to Kill

Allosaurus was a formidable predator. Its skull alone was some 3 feet (1 m) long, with large "windows" instead of bony slabs forming passages for tissues and muscle attachment sites. The curved serrated teeth were up to four inches (10 cm) long. The neck was strong, not unlike a bulldog's, the body muscular, the hands three-fingered with curving claws, and the powerful legs each equipped with three strong-clawed toes and one toe (the first) smaller, set higher, and to the side of the foot.

AUSTRALIAN ALLOSAUR?

Virtually all *Allosaurus* fossils have been found in North America. However, there are possible remains from Portugal in Europe, from Mtwara in Tanzania, East Africa, and also from Cape Patterson, Victoria, Australia. The Australian evidence is based mainly on one specimen, an astragalus (ankle bone) from the Early Cretaceous, as well as a claw fragment and partial vertebrae. The astragalus is allosaurlike but small, and may be attributed to a relative rather than *Allosaurus* itself.

A hungry *Allosaurus* attacks a young, struggling *Diplodocus*. Some experts believe that *Allosaurus* may have hunted in groups, which may have been capable of bringing down even massive adult sauropods.

King of Dinosaurs

For almost all of the twentieth century, *Tyrannosaurus rex* was regarded as the largest meat-eater ever to walk the Earth. Until this Late Cretaceous colossus was usurped as

years earlier by Barnum Brown at Hell Creek, Dawson County, northern Montana. In 1908, Brown excavated a more complete skeleton from the same area, allowing more confident reconstructions of the great carnivore. *Tyrannosaurus* took its place as the megastar of the dinosaur world, with leading

largest carnivorous dinosaur by the likes of *Spinosaurus* and *Giganotosaurus*, the "king tyrant lizard" captured popular imagination as almost no other creature before or since.

Tyrannosaurus was first described for science in 1905 by the American Museum of Natural History's Henry Fairfield Osborn (1857–1935) from a partial skeleton discovered three

More than 50 serrated teeth and a mouth big enough to swallow an adult human allowed *Tyrannosaurus rex*, one of the most massive predators who ever lived, to devour its meals in short order.

roles in innumerable stories, magazine series, and movies such as the *Jurassic Park* series of the 1990s.

The Arrival of "Sue"

In 1990, fossil-hunting Sue Hendrickson came upon some large remains at a dig site near Faith, South Dakota. They were soon recognized as a large *Tyrannosaurus*, and excavations proceeded with great excitement. The result was "Sue," one of the world's best known fossil specimens, nicknamed for its discoverer. In 2000, Sue was unveiled by the Field Museum, Chicago, as one of the biggest and best preserved *Tyrannosaurus* fossils yet found.

Sue has awesome vital statistics. Measuring 42 feet (12.8 m) in length and 13 feet (4 m) high at the hips, Sue would have weighed up to 7 tons. The skull itself is 5 feet (1.5 m) long; the largest of the 58 serrated teeth measures almost 12 inches (30 cm). Despite its nickname, the sex of Sue is uncertain.

How Did *Tyrannosaurus* Hunt?

Great discussions have taken place over the lifestyle and hunting methods of *Tyrannosaurus*. From skeletal evidence and biomechanical calculations, some authorities contend that this immense carnivore was too heavy and lumbering to be fleet of foot, with a

TEENAGE GROWTH SPURT

In 2004, U.S. scientists published evidence for a greatly increased rate of development during *Tyrannosaurus'* teenage years. The claims were based on growth lines detectable in the fossil bones of more than 20 *Tyrannosaurus* and similar dinosaurs, including *Albertosaurus* and *Daspletosaurus*. The study suggested that in some specimens of *Tyrannosaurus*, weight gain was more than 4 pounds (2 kg) every day between the ages of 14 and 18 years.

top short sprint speed of 20–25 miles per hour (32–40 km/h). So it probably adopted a primarily scavenging role, feasting on carcasses of animals that had died from natural causes or perhaps picking off the young, old, or ill. Or it was an ambush specialist, bursting upon prey with a short dash. But the size and proportions of the rear leg bones, and the nature of their joints, work against an active predation scenario.

What is much more certain are the size and strength of *Tyrannosaurus'* forequarters. Its massive skull is deep, with a gape widened by flexible joints along the lower jaw. The huge teeth, strong skull structure, and flexible yet powerful neck were well able to cope with the shocks and stresses of struggling prey.

A New "King"

In 1995, the "tyrant lizard king" *Tyrannosaurus rex* lost its crown as the largest carnivorous dinosaur and the biggest terrestrial meat-eater of all time. Argentinean paleontologists Rodolfo Coria and Leonardo Salgado announced an even more monstrous predator, *Giganotosaurus carolinii*, "Carolini's giant southern lizard."

Relationships

Giganotosaurus was a tetanuran ("stiff- tailed") theropod. Its skeletal remains were amazingly more than 70 percent complete, and showed that it had much in common with large carnivores of the allosaur type, such as the African *Carcharodontosaurus* and North American *Acrocanthosaurus*, both from the mid-Cretaceous, as well as *Allosaurus*, from the Jurassic Period. A second, even bigger specimen of *Giganotosaurus* was also located, some 8 percent larger than the first. Although it was less complete, it confirmed the bulky dimensions of this huge carnivore.

One of the largest known carnivores ever to walk the Earth, the aptly named *Giganotosaurus* may have fed on some of the world's largest sauropods, such as *Argentinosaurus*.

Outsizing the "King"

Giganotosaurus is estimated at some 45 feet (13.7 m) long, 12 feet (3.7 m) tall at the hips, and perhaps 18 feet (5.5 m) high at the head, weighing 6 tons or more (some estimates go as heavy as 8 tons). Such dimensions are larger all around than those of *Tyrannosaurus*. For example, the femur (thigh bone) of *Giganotosaurus* is 2 inches (5 cm) longer than its rival's equivalent.

The skull of *Giganotosaurus* has been compared to a bathtub in size, about 6 feet (1.8 m) in length, with serrated teeth up to 10 inches (20 cm).

Cretaceous Argentina

Giganotosaurus lived during the Early Late Cretaceous Period, 100–90 million years ago, predating *Tyrannosaurus* by more than 25 million years. Despite its greater linear dimensions, its skull is not as heavily constructed as that of *Tyrannosaurus*. Its teeth are not quite as sizeable and are also more knife-like rather than elongated cones as in *Tyrannosaurus*. Perhaps *Giganotosaurus* was not as sturdy and strong as *Tyrannosaurus* when it came to tackling prey that might fight back.

The brain cavity of *Giganotosaurus* is smaller than that of *Tyrannosaurus* and shaped more like a long, narrow banana, rather than being wide and high. The region of the brain dealing with the sense of smell, known as the olfactory lobe, is relatively large, showing that *Giganotosaurus* could sniff its way around the environment.

Titanic Struggle

What type of food might *Giganotosaurus* have consumed? Fossils found near its site from approximately the same time include the long-necked plant-eating dinosaurs called titanosaurs (from the sauropod group). There is evidence for the presence of the titanosaur *Argentinosaurus*, which was possibly the biggest dinosaur and largest land animal of all time. It is convenient to assume that the giant carnivore hunted the mountainous herbivore, although it is hard to imagine fossil finds that would lend firm evidence for such a battle of the giants.

EVERLASTING FAME

Giganotosaurus' species name *carolinii* honors car mechanic and part-time fossil sleuth Ruben Carolini. In 1993, he was surveying the windy rock-strewn landscape about 50 miles (80 km) from Plaza Huincul, in Argentina's Neuquén province. Carolini spotted some promisingly massive remains near the village of El Chocón and soon contacted Coria at the local Museo Carmen Funes (Carmen Funes Museum) in Plaza Huincul.

The "Dinosaur Shark"

Perhaps the most feared creature in today's oceans is the great white shark, *Carcharodon carcharias*, itself a record holder as the world's biggest living predatory fish. Part of its scientific name has been applied to a huge carnivorous dinosaur that competes with the likes *Tyrannosaurus*, *Giganotosaurus*, and *Spinosaurus* as the largest land predator of all time. This is *Carcharodontosaurus*, the "shark-tooth lizard."

Carcharodontosaurus fossils come from northern Africa, especially Egypt, Morocco, and Niger, with possible finds also in Tunisia, Algeria, and Libya. They indicate a large, heavily built theropod, similar in many ways to *Giganotosaurus*, that prowled what is now the Sahara region some 100–90 million years ago. At that time, the Early Late Cretaceous Period, the landscape of North Africa was very different from today. There were low-lying mosaics of swamps, pools, river courses, and gentle hills, well cloaked with vegetation. In some areas the sea made incursions, forming coastal habitats.

Carcharodontosaurus is estimated in the range of 40 to 45 feet (12.2–13.6 m) long, with a hip height of 12 feet (3.6 m). The size, proportions, and sturdy nature of its bones suggest a weight of 4 to 5 tons. The skull is estimated at

SPECIFICATIONS

Dinosaur: *Carcharodontosaurus*
Meaning: Shark-tooth lizard
Order: Saurischia
Family: Carcharodontosauridae
Period: Cretaceous
Size: 46–49 feet (14–15 m) long, 7–8 tons
First discovered: 1927, Sahara Desert. Named by Ernst Stromer von Reichenbach in 1931
Region: Northern Africa
Characteristics:
- Rivals the *Giganotosaurus* as the largest meat-eating creature to walk the Earth
- 5-foot (1.5 m) long skull, as tall as some present day humans
- Outweighs present-day great white sharks by 10 times
- Razor-sharp triangular teeth, some of which can measure up to 8 inches (20 cm) long

a little more than 5 feet (1.5 m) in length, with powerful jaws and sharp, serrated teeth up to 8 inches (20 cm) long.

Curious Coincidences

The story of *Carcharodontosaurus* has several strange twists. Some of its fossils were excavated from Egypt in 1927 and identified as *Megalosaurus*, specifically *M. saharicus*. As explained previously, at the time *Megalosaurus* was a name applied to many large meat-eating dinosaurs.

The remains were transported from Egypt to the Bavarian State Collection of Paleontology and Geology in Munich, Germany. In

> "*Carcharodontosaurus* was named "for its mainly *Carcharodon* [great white shark]-like teeth . . . not recurved, almost bilaterally symmetrical but with convex edges."
> —ERNST STROMER VON REICHENBACH, 1931.

1931, Ernst Stromer von Reichenbach (1870–1952) studied them and reassigned them to a new genus, *Carcharodontosaurus*. But in 1944 a World War II Allied bombing raid hit the collections. The fossils were destroyed, although Stromer's descriptions and illustrations remained in the scientific literature. Without physical objects to examine and compare with new finds, *Carcharodontosaurus* went into limbo.

Fast-forward to 1995–96. University of Chicago paleontologist Paul Sereno (b. 1957) and his teams uncovered the remains of a big theropod in Morocco. Searching the literature, they were struck by the likeness of the teeth and skull to Stromer's scientific descriptions of the Egyptian *Carcharodontosaurus*

from more than 60 years earlier. The new find was larger, but so similar that it, too, was named *Carcharodontosaurus*.

Paleontologist Paul Sereno shows off the 5-foot-long (1.5 m) skull and the massive teeth of a mid-Cretaceous *Carcharodontosaurus*, discovered in the Sahara Desert.

Sail in the Sunset

Below: Despite its alarming size and appearance, some experts posit that the diet of *Spinosaurus* consisted largely of scavenged meat and fish.

Opposite: Its distinctively long snout, reminiscent of that of a crocodile, places *Spinosaurus* in a select group of theropods.

In 2006, a scientific report suggested that *Spinosaurus*, "spine (thorny) lizard" was the largest of all the carnivorous dinosaurs and deserved the title of greatest meat-eater ever to walk the Earth. However *Spinosaurus* was not a new discovery. What had changed was the study of newly obtained specimens and reassessment of an old favorite.

Spinosaurus was named in 1915 by German paleontologist Ernst Stromer von Reichenbach from material uncovered in 1912 in Bahariya Valley, Egypt. Stromer knew he had found a huge theropod, very long—he estimated 60 feet (18.3 m)—but more lightly built than *Tyrannosaurus*.

The fossils were stored in Munich, Germany. But they were destroyed by an Allied bombing raid in World War II, just like those of the previously described *Carcharodontosaurus*. During the 1990s, more remains similar to *Spinosaurus* came to light, all originating in earlier years from Morocco. A portion of skull bone from the snout was acquired from a private collector and pieces of upper rear skull from the University of Chicago Museum. This gathered evidence, along with Stromer's original descriptions, was surveyed by paleontologist Cristiano Dal Sasso of Milan's Museo Civico di Storia Naturale (Civic Natural History Museum) and colleagues. They concluded that *Spinosaurus* was indeed the biggest dinosaurian carnivore.

Crocodilian Dinosaur

Estimates for the size of *Spinosaurus* vary greatly, but are in the range of 49 to 56 feet (15–17 m) for length and from 4 to 8 tons in weight. In form, *Spinosaurus* differed from other large theropods in being slimmer and lighter in general build. It also had tall spinelike extensions to the vertebrae (backbones) from the shoulders to the hips. Some of these straplike spines are almost 6 feet (1.8 m) long.

The snout of *Spinosaurus* is low and long, and the jaws somewhat crocodilian. Distinctively, the teeth have no or few serrations and are generally conical and pointed, but hardly curved. Again, this is reminiscent of a crocodile. Other meat-eaters placed in the *Spinosaurus* group include *Baryonyx* from England and *Suchomimus* from Niger.

As described earlier, the Cretaceous habitat of *Spinosaurus*, 95–90 million years ago, was quite unlike North Africa today. Wetlands, pools, and river channels crossed the land, and the climate was moist and tropical. Some strands of evidence, such as a swordfish vertebra stuck next to a spinosaur tooth, suggest that *Spinosaurus* may have fished in the pools and creeks, seizing prey in the shallows with a lunge of its massive, sharp-toothed mouth.

WHY THE SAIL?

The tall bony extensions on the back vertebrae of *Spinosaurus* have long been the subject of speculation. Such features are known from other dinosaurs such as the iguanodontian *Ouranosaurus*, which lived a few million years earlier than *Spinosaurus*, also in North Africa (Niger). The extensions may have supported a moundlike ridge of flesh or a "sail" of skin. Among the numerous suggestions for the functions of a back sail are:

- Body temperature control. The sail's large surface area would absorb the Sun's heat, which the animal's blood could then spread around the body, thus allowing *Spinosaurus* to become active quickly, for example, at daybreak. If the reptile became overheated, then standing in the shade with the sail at right angles to the breeze would help it to lose body heat.
- Some kind of visual symbol or display. A brightly colored, patterned sail might intimidate possible enemies or discourage breeding rivals and impress partners at mating time.

CHAPTER 2

BIGGEST PLANT-EATERS

THE ACCOLADE OF "BIGGEST ANIMAL THAT EVER LIVED" is often awarded to the giant of today's oceans, the blue whale. Commonly quoted maximums for this vast mammal are 100 feet (30.5 m) in length and 150 tons in weight. Many specimens of the largest living land animal—the African bush (or savannah) elephant—exceed 5 tons and, rarely, males weigh in at more than 10 tons.

For many decades the title of "biggest dinosaur," and most massive land animal ever, was held by the Late Jurassic sauropod *Brachiosaurus*. Indeed, all of the very lengthy, very bulky dinosaurs come from the long-necked, long-tailed, herbivorous sauropod group. *Brachiosaurus* was far heavier than an elephant—perhaps even six elephants—but not as weighty as the blue whale. *Brachiosaurus* also long held the honor of the tallest-ever land animal, at more than twice the height of a giraffe.

In recent years, as with the carnivorous dinosaurs, exciting discoveries have shown that *Brachiosaurus* was probably not the largest or tallest dinosaur. South America has yielded tantalizing remains of what were even more massive moving mountains of flesh and bone, including *Argentinosaurus* and *Puertasaurus*. Other giants include *Sauroposeidon* and *Seismosaurus*.

A sauropod of the Late Jurassic, *Barosaurus* measured 89 feet (27 m) from head to tail tip; much of this length belonged to its tail and neck. Here a *Barosaurus* skeleton nearly scrapes the ceiling inside the American Museum of Natural History in New York City.

The "Dinosaur Giraffe"

The world's tallest living animal, the giraffe, browses acacias and other trees in Africa's mixed woodland and savannah. Its extremely elongated neck, coupled with very long front limbs, and its lengthy grasping tongue, allow this mammal to reach leaves almost 20 feet (6 m) above the ground. But the giraffe would be put into the shade by a huge dinosaur from the Late Jurassic Period, *Brachiosaurus* ("arm lizard"). Its browsing height, estimated from a relatively complete composite skeleton, was 42 feet (12.8 m). Some isolated skeletal parts are even larger, suggesting that this vast herbivore raised its head to a height exceeding 45 feet (13.7 m).

Brachiosaurus is well known from numerous fossil remains, although these may represent two or more species within the genus. The dinosaur was first described in 1900 by Elmer S.

Brachiosaurus had a distinctive profile, with a sloping back from the discrepancy between its long front legs and shorter hind legs.

Riggs (1869–1963) from an incomplete skeleton excavated at Grand River Canyon, Colorado. At first, Riggs assumed that the longer limb bones were in the rear legs, as with other sauropods. Initially, he identified the humerus (upper foreleg bone) as the femur (upper hind-leg or thigh bone).

Discovery in East Africa

In 1907, mineral prospectors in German East Africa, now Tanzania, discovered enormous fossil bones at Tendaguru, a site near Lindi and Mtwara. Fossil reptile expert Eberhard Fraas (1862–1916) happened to be in the region, visited the site, and at once recognized its significance. News reached Berlin, where an ambitious expedition was promptly organized by the Museum für Naturkunde (described in chapter 13). Fossils excavated from East Africa included fine remains of *Brachiosaurus* and also of the stegosaur *Kentrosaurus*, the meat-eater *Elaphrosaurus*, and many others. Assembling the evidence from various skeletons, scientists determined that *Brachiosaurus* probably attained a length of 82 feet (25 m, by

SPECIFICATIONS

Dinosaur: _Brachiosaurus_
Meaning: Arm Reptile
Order: Saurischia
Family: Brachiosauridae
Period: Late Jurassic
Size: 82 feet (25 m) long, 50–80 tons
First discovered: 1903, Grand River Canyon, by
    Elmer Riggs
Region: Midwestern United States, Africa
Characteristics:
- One of the tallest dinosaurs discovered to the present day
- Even though the mouth contained over 50 teeth, it is believed that this dinosaur swallowed its food whole. The food was later digested in the stomach.
- Quadruped; front legs longer that the hind legs
- Nasal passages located at the top of the head

Being so tall would allow _Brachiosaurus_ to browse conifers, ginkgoes, cycads, and other trees at a higher level than other herbivores, thereby avoiding competition for food. However, as discussed later, _Brachiosaurus_ may not have been able to lift its head very high because of the heartbeat power (blood pressure) needed to send blood up to the brain.

Old reconstructions of _Brachiosaurus_ show a semiaquatic animal, grazing while almost submerged, using its long neck as a snorkel-like breathing tube. This idea arose from the position of the nasal openings, which are on top of the skull, above and in front of the eyes. But features of the rib cage and limbs, and physical calculations, show water pressure would have prevented the dinosaur from breathing. Consequently, the semiaquatic speculation has long been discounted.

no means a dinosaurian record). It had a relatively short tail for a sauropod, but its neck was enormously long (although, again, not a dinosaurian record). The long front limbs and back sloping down to the shorter hind legs gave a vaguely giraffelike profile. For many years weight estimates of 60, 70, or even 80 tons were common for _Brachiosaurus_. However, more recent approximations are in the region of 30–40 tons, with a few isolated fossils hinting at larger individuals of possibly more than 50 tons.

Why was _Brachiosaurus_ not only so huge, but also so tall? Increased size, with the strength and weight it brings, provides defense against predators.

Much like modern-day giraffes, it is thought that _Brachiosaurus_ used its extreme height to collect much of its food from treetops which were out of reach for most other species. Its teeth were perfectly suited for pulling leaves from branches.

Land of Giants

Sauropod dinosaurs, which consist of several main groups, share common features, such as a small head, long neck and tail, barrel-like body, and columnar legs. The titanosaurs were poorly known for many years, beginning with very limited remains described as *Titanosaurus* in 1877 by English naturalist and geologist Richard Lydekker (1849–1915). Until recently, the Late Cretaceous *Saltasaurus*, from Argentina's Salta province, was one of the best represented. Described and named in 1980, it was some 39 feet (11.9 m) in length, with an estimated weight of 7 tons, and may have had bony plates embedded in its skin for self-defense.

A series of exciting discoveries have since characterized the titanosaur group as numerous and widespread—and the last major group of sauropods to appear and diversify. It includes the biggest animals ever to walk the Earth. Titanosaurs occupied southern continents during the Cretaceous and also spread into Asia (*Euhelopus* and others) and Europe (*Ampelosaurus*, *Magyarosaurus*). The most spectacular finds have been in South America; eminent among them is the vast "Argentina lizard," *Argentinosaurus*.

Part of the sauropod group, *Argentinosaurus* was one of the largest of the titanosaurs. It is estimated to have weighed more than 60 tons.

Argentine Finds

Only about one-twentieth of the skeleton of *Argentinosaurus* is known. These remains include bits of ribs, several vertebrae (backbones), and parts of the sacrum (the fused vertebrae that are part of the hip bone), and the tibia (lower rear-leg bone). They were excavated near Plaza Huincul in Argentina's Neuquén province, beginning in 1987. *Argentinosaurus* was described and named in 1993 by José Bonaparte and Rodolfo Coria. The fossils are dated to approximately 100–90 million years

ago. This particular specimen of *Argentinosaurus* seemed to have ended up in a fast-flowing stream that spread its bones over a wide area, as indicated by the pebbles incorporated into the sandstone in which the fossils were embedded.

Despite the limited evidence, the fossils' sizes and features can be compared with the same skeletal parts in similar titanosaurs and then scaled up to produce estimates of the complete animal. Vertebrae more than 5 feet (1.5 m) in both height and width indicate a colossal creature. The vertebrae

SPECIFICATIONS

Dinosaur: *Argentinosaurus*
Meaning: Argentina Lizard
Order: Saurischia
Family: Titanosauridae
Period: Late Cretaceous
Size: 80–100 feet (24–30 m) long, 60–70 tons
First discovered: Argentina
Region: South America
Characteristics:
- At the present time this is the largest dinosaur known
- Backbone vertebrae could be as large as 5 feet (1.5 m) tall and 5 feet (1.5 m) wide
- Quadruped
- Herbivore

were partly hollow, yet also distinctively and strongly interlocked in the back, thus providing strength with lightness.

Prey and Predator

The remains of the huge meat-eater *Giganotosaurus* were found not far from the fossils of *Argentinosaurus*. Although separated in time by several million years, it is tempting to speculate that these two giants, or their close relatives, may have come face to face as hungry predator and potential prey. Exactly why this region saw an "evolutionary size race" in the Cretaceous Period, with both predator and prey increasing in bulk and power, is unknown. Whatever its exact size, *Argentinosaurus* was certainly a giant among titans.

More Southern Titans

The year 2006 saw the announcement of a huge sauropod that might rival *Argentinosaurus* for the title of biggest dinosaur and largest-ever land animal. This was *Puertasaurus*, a titanosaur like *Argentinosaurus*, but from much later in the Cretaceous Period—near its end, only 70–65 million years ago. Its full genus and species names are *Puertasaurus reuili*, in honor of the fossil hunters who found and prepared the specimens, Pablo Puerta and Santiago Reuil. The remains were located near La Leona in Santa Cruz province, Argentina, in gray sandstone that also contained fossilized conifers, cycads, and other vegetation.

Revealing Backbones

The evidence for *Puertasaurus* centers on four vertebrae. These include most of a cervical (neck) vertebra, one complete dorsal vertebra from the forward part of the main back near the shoulders, and the central portions of two caudal (tail) vertebrae. Not only is their immensity striking—the neck vertebra measures 46 inches (118 cm) from front to back, and 55 inches (140 cm) from side to side, while the dorsal

Yet another colossal dinosaur found in Argentina, *Puertasaurus* lived some 70 million years ago. Paleontologist Fernando Novas and his team researched and described its remains in 2006.

vertebra is 42 inches (106 cm) tall and an amazing 66 inches (168 cm) from side to side—the shapes of the bones are also distinctive, being lower and wider than in most other titanosaurs.

Standard practice with such limited remains compares their sizes and shapes with the equivalent parts of smaller but better-known titanosaurs, and then scales up the whole beast to an approximation of its adult size. The results here were truly extreme. *Puertasaurus* was an estimated 100 feet (30.5 m) in length, and roughly 80 tons in weight. Thus it rivalled or even exceeded *Argentinosaurus* in overall size, although the two lived some 20 million years apart. Of course these sizes are estimates from very limited fossil evidence and await further finds for confirmation or revision.

Tidal Giant

Fossils of the titanosaur *Paralititan* originate from the locality known as Bahariya, in the Western Desert south of Cairo, Egypt. In this area in the 1910s, German paleontologist Ernst Stromer von Reichenbach recovered fossils of dinosaurs such as the massive carnivore *Spinosaurus*. One of the most precious fossil bones of *Paralititan* is the humerus (upper arm bone), with a length of 66 inches (169 cm). Applying the scaling rules and extrapolating to the whole dinosaur, *Paralititan* was probably in the range of 65 to 80 feet (20–24.4 m) long and tipped the scales at 70 to 80 tons.

Longer, Heavier

For many, the sauropod *Diplodocus* typifies a big plant-eating dinosaur: tiny head, elongated neck, tubby body, stumpy legs, and enormously lengthy, whiplike tail. For many years *Diplodocus* was the biggest known dinosaur and land animal. Its remains first came to light in 1878 at the famous fossil site of Como Bluff, Wyoming. The great reptile was named two years later by eminent paleontologist Othniel Charles Marsh; *Diplodocus* means "double beam," referring to the two skidlike chevron bones projecting front and rear on the underside of some caudal (tail) vertebrae in the middle section of the tail. Marsh saw this as a distinctive trait although it has since been noted in other sauropods.

All Neck and Tail

Diplodocus may not hold many records today, having been supplanted in weight, length, and other measurements by later discoveries. But at the time it caused a sensation. Its various fossils provide a virtually complete skeletal picture—indeed, it remains the longest

Diplodocus fossils such as this skull are approximately 150–145 million years old. A relatively large number of *Diplodocus* remains have been recovered over the years.

dinosaur known from a complete skeleton, at 89 feet (27 m). But this is largely neck, at 26 feet (8 m), and the 70-plus vertebrae of the tail, stretching 45 feet (13.7 m). Early estimates of weight were 20 or even 30 tons. But *Diplodocus* was slim, even slight, compared with sauropods such as brachiosaurs and titanosaurs; more recent estimates put its weight at 15 to 25 tons. Its fossils, dated to the Late Jurassic (generally 150–145 million years ago), are found in Colorado, Wyoming, and Utah.

The skull of *Diplodocus* has fringes of peg-shaped teeth around the front of the upper and lower jaws, but no rear teeth. The dinosaur probably used these like two opposed garden rakes to strip leaves and other vegetation, which were swallowed unchewed.

Getting Heavier

Great confusion surrounded fossils named as *Atlantosaurus*, *Apatosaurus*, and *Brontosaurus*. Remains of these huge sauropods were excavated from Colorado and Wyoming and described by Othniel Charles Marsh. *Atlantosaurus* and *Apatosaurus* were early namings in 1877; fossils discovered later were dubbed *Brontosaurus* in 1879. Further studies, however, showed that some of these had been misidentified. It became something of a naming nightmare.

"Most Colossal Animal Ever on Earth Just Found Out West."

—1898 *New York World* newspaper headline (inspired industrialist Andrew Carnegie to support the search for *Diplodocus* and other fossils)

Over the following years, the tangle was gradually sorted out. By convention, if newly discovered fossils are ascribed to one genus and/or species, but it then becomes clear they actually belong to an existing, already described genus and/or species, the first name takes precedence. So all *Brontosaurus* specimens reverted to the name *Apatosaurus*, and the name *Brontosaurus* was deleted from official dinosaur lists. *Brontosaurus* (which means "thunder lizard"), though, had become such a star in popular culture that for many decades its name proved difficult to eradicate.

Apatosaurus ("deceptive lizard") is well known from finds in Colorado, Oklahoma, Utah, and Wyoming. It was a contemporary and cousin of *Diplodocus* but shorter and sturdier, 69 to 75 feet

SPECIFICATIONS

Dinosaur: *Diplodocus*
Meaning: Double Beam
Order: Saurischia
Family: Diplodocidae
Period: Late Jurassic
Size: 89 feet (27.1 m) long, 15–25 tons
First discovered: 1877, Como Bluff, Wyoming, by S. W. Williston
Region: North America
Characteristics:
• Peglike teeth only in front of the mouth
• Tail had extra anvil-shaped support bones

(21–23 m) in length, with a relatively shorter neck but an extremely elongated tail, and a weight of 25 to 35 tons. As with *Diplodocus* and other "long-necks," there is great debate about how flexible their necks really were in life and how high the head could be raised, as outlined on later pages.

An illustration of an *Apatosaurus* traveling through water. Scientists once hypothesized that *Apatosaurus* lived partially submerged in water to help support its massive frame. This theory was later discounted, and it is thought that they lived and grazed on land like other sauropods.

A Confusion of Names

In 1991, the biggest-ever dinosaur spotlight fell upon another outsized sauropod, with the announcement of *Seismosaurus* ("ground-shaking/earthquake lizard"). Initial size estimates were stupendous: up to 170 feet (52 m) long, with a weight of 120 tons. The fossils, discovered in New Mexico, comprising parts of vertebrae, pelvis (hip bone), and ribs, were dated to the Late Jurassic Period.

Further studies of *Seismosaurus* have not borne out its initial record-breaking promise. The position of the caudal (tail) vertebrae was revised, moving them from the middle of the tail to nearer the hips, where larger dimensions would be expected. This "shrank" *Seismosaurus* in length to 100–110 feet (30–33 m). As a close cousin of the slimline *Diplodocus*, its weight was reduced to 20–25 tons. In fact, its similarity to *Diplodocus* suggested that *Seismosaurus* may well be a large specimen within this genus. It may deserve the new species name of *Diplodocus hallorum*—or even be included in the existing largest *Diplodocus* species, *D. longus*.

Super and Ultra

In 1972, huge dinosaur bones were unearthed at Dry Mesa Quarry, Colorado, and studied by American paleontologist James Jensen (1918–98). In one find, a spectacular scapulocoracoid (shoulder bone), taller than an adult human, plus some

TALLEST?

Brachiosaurus was certainly tall (see earlier discussion). In 1994, four huge cervical (neck) vertebrae were uncovered in Atoka county, Oklahoma. Their study in 1999 suggested an even taller sauropod, which was named *Sauroposeidon* ("Poseidon lizard") in 2000. (In addition to the sea, the ancient Greek god Poseidon was associated with earthquakes and ground-shaking, hence the link to a heavily plodding giant dinosaur.) *Sauroposeidon* might have craned its neck and head to stand 50 feet (15.2 m) tall—as high as a six-story building. Its weight is estimated at 50 tons and its length at 88–98 feet (27–30 m). *Sauroposeidon*, dated at 110 million years ago, lived in the Cretaceous Period, later than most other brachiosaurs. It may have been North America's last giant sauropod.

cervical vertebrae (neck backbones), and other remains signified a sauropod that was perhaps 130 feet (40 m) in length. In 1985, Jensen named the find *Ultrasaurus* ("extreme/ultra lizard"). But it transpired that this name was already in use, for a brachiosaurlike dinosaur whose fossils had been found in South Korea and named in 1983. So, in 1991, *Ultrasaurus* swapped its last "u" for an "o" and became *Ultrasauros*.

As sometimes happens in paleontology, further studies showed that the *Ultrasauros* remains were probably a mix of two dinosaurs. One was a likely *Brachiosaurus*, which owned the shoulder bone. Fossils of the other were from a *Diplodocus* type of sauropod that Jensen had already named *Supersaurus* ("super lizard") from other specimens found earlier in 1972 at the same quarry. Since *Supersaurus* was the first name assigned, it took precedence, and *Ultrasauros* was discontinued.

In another twist to the tale, the South Korean *Ultrasaurus* is also in limbo. Reassessment of its remains show that it was smaller than originally thought, and the fossils are too limited to assign it with confidence to any new or existing genus.

A *Supersaurus* shoulder bone measuring some 6 feet (1.8 m) and other fragments from this gargantuan dinosaur were discovered in Colorado in 1972. More recently, *Supersaurus* bones were unearthed in central Wyoming.

Why So Big?

The largest land animal today is the African bush (savannah) elephant, with males occasionally exceeding 10 tons. Excluding dinosaurs, the largest land animal that ever lived was probably a mammal, *Indricotherium* (formerly *Baluchitherium*, and possibly the same as *Paraceratherium*). This giant hornless rhino roamed Asia during the Oligocene epoch, about 30–25 million years ago. It was up to 27 feet (8.2 m) from nose to tail, 17 feet (5.2 m) tall at the head, and weighed between 10 and 15 tons.

Yet during the Jurassic and Cretaceous Periods, a wide array of dinosaurs from the sauropod group grew far larger, with many weighing 20 tons and a number exceeding 50 tons. Why did these dinosaurs grow so huge? Was it an inherent feature of their group or more linked to the climate, habitats, and other conditions of the time?

The short reply is that there is no simple answer. But there are various proposals, and perhaps a combination of them applies.

- Great size, coupled with overwhelming bulk and muscle power, probably helped with self-defense against predators—especially carnivorous theropod dinosaurs, which also grew to huge proportions in the "evolutionary size race."

- A typical sauropod's long neck may have enabled it to browse high in trees, thereby avoiding competition with herbivores feeding at lower levels. (Although how high these dinosaurs could actually raise their heads is debated, as described later.)

- A bulky body can house a large digestive system, holding more food for longer periods of time. This encourages effective digestion, especially of tough, low-nutrient plant matter that needs time to break down.

- A big creature can store proportionally more energy reserves and water in body tissues (fat and muscle) than a smaller animal. This helps it to survive periods of famine or drought.

- The rate of heat loss or gain from a body decreases as the body gets larger, because the proportion of surface area, where heat exchange occurs, lessens compared with volume, where heat is stored. Large living "cold-blooded" reptiles such as crocodiles, big turtles, and komodo dragon lizards maintain a generally higher and more constant body temperature than do smaller reptiles. This allows more efficient metabolism, greater activity, and increased energy conservation. Huge dinosaurs may have had a much greater degree of this so-called thermal inertia and thus maintained a higher body temperature, a phenomenon dubbed "gigantothermy."

• Warm moist climates, less marked seasons, and different levels of atmospheric gases, including more oxygen, perhaps contributed to faster Mesozoic plant growth compared with modern times. Recent studies show that vegetation grew up to three times more quickly then than similar plants do today, providing more food for herbivores.

• Many reptiles today grow rapidly when young; the growth rate slows progressively as they reach adulthood and old age. Reptile speed of growth depends more on food supply than it does in, for example, mammals, which tend to enlarge at a more predetermined rate. Reptiles such as crocodiles usually grow faster and reach greater adult size if better fed. Maybe some dinosaurs, surrounded by copious foodstuffs, did the same.

The dinosaurs' world was very different from our modern environment. Perhaps a mix of climate, food supplies, predatory threats, and body temperature control encouraged them to become extreme in size—the most colossal creatures ever to walk our planet.

A herd of *Apatosaurus* eats its way through a grove of trees, watched by a lone *Ceratosaurus*. While there is no clear evidence as to what made sauropods so big, certain factors such as climate and an abundant food supply certainly contributed to their development.

CHAPTER 3

SMALL AND DAINTY

NOT ALL DINOSAURS WERE VAST BEASTS, shaking the ground with their pounding strides. At the other extreme of the size spectrum, the most diminutive dinosaurs were, or rather are, as long as a thumb, with a sharp beak and wings. Birds evolved from dinosaurs and so are considered to be part of the dinosaur group or clade. (A clade consists of the most recent common ancestor of a set of organisms and all the descendants of that common ancestor.) Technically, the smallest dinosaur is the littlest bird. This is the bee hummingbird of Cuba, just 2.5 inches (6.4 cm) from beak to tail and weighing only 0.06 ounces (1.7 g).

In the case of nonavian dinosaurs, for many years the most diminutive known was *Compsognathus*. ("Smallest" here refers, of course, to the adult, not to hatchlings or juveniles.) But, as with the title of the biggest, recent finds have entered more and more contenders for the honor of being the smallest. They were mostly slim and slightly built, being mainly neck, legs, and tail. Some of these pint-sized creatures would be barely knee-high to a human. These little reptiles appear to have been fast and agile. They could probably scamper into undergrowth or squeeze between rocks as they avoided predators and searched for food.

A pair of *Microraptor zhaoianus*, measuring only 2 feet (60 cm) in length, chatter to each other. Researchers believe that these feathered dinosaurs swooped with their forelimbs held higher than their hind limbs.

Pretty Small

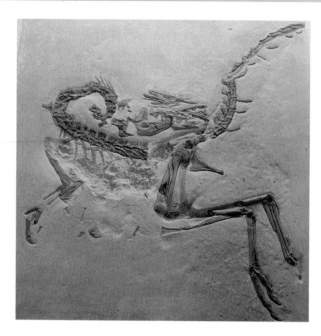

A small hunter of the Late Jurassic, both known specimens of *Compsognathus longipes* include the remains of lizard dinners in the stomachs, giving a clear clue to its diet.

One was excavated at Solnhofen in the 1850s; it has the distinction of being the first dinosaur described and named from a relatively complete skeleton—by Johann Wagner in 1859. However, it was not recognized as dinosaurian until 35 years later when examined by Othniel Charles Marsh. A reappraisal of the evidence in 1978 by John Ostrom brought "Compy" into the spotlight as the smallest (nonavian) dinosaur. The reappraisal included a second specimen found in 1972 near Nice, France.

Slim and Trim

The German *Compsognathus*, probably a juvenile, measures about 35 inches (89 cm) in length, while the French specimen is more mature at almost 50 inches (127 cm). At first these two finds were given different species names, *C. longipes* and *C. corallestris*, respectively, but both are now usually regarded as *C. longipes*. The very slim build and proportions, with more than half the length being slender tail, gave a total weight of about 6–7 pounds (3 kg).

Compsognathus was remarkably birdlike in many features. Indeed, some fossils of *Archaeopteryx* were labeled as *Compsognathus* until restudy showed their true significance. *Compsognathus* had hollow bones, a long narrow head with a pointed snout, long jaws with

The limestone deposits around Solnhofen in Bavaria, southern Germany, are famed for their plentiful and amazingly well-preserved fossils. This fine-grained limestone has captured the tiny anatomical details of many plants and animals. From here come exquisite remains of the reptilelike fliers known as pterosaurs, the earliest known bird, *Archaeopteryx*, and one of the smallest of all nonavian dinosaurs, *Compsognathus* ("elegant jaw"). For decades this theropod, in the same large group as the great meat-eaters such as *Tyrannosaurus*, was regarded as the smallest known dinosaur.

Compsognathus is known mainly from two fairly complete specimens.

SPECIFICATIONS

Dinosaur: *Compsognathus*
Meaning: Elegant Jaw
Order: Saurischia
Family: Compsognathidae
Period: Late Jurassic
Size: 4–7 feet (1–2 m) long, 6.5 pounds (3 kg)
First discovered: Late 1850s, Bavaria, Germany,
  by Dr. Joseph Oberndorfer
Region: Germany and France
Characteristics:
- Roughly the same size as a chicken; considered to be one of the smallest dinosaurs yet discovered
- Bipedal carnivore; had two long, lean legs with three-toed feet
- Sported a long tail which provided balance and support
- Long neck and small head, with small, sharp teeth

tiny sharp teeth, a long flexible neck, a lean trim body, longish arms with two or three clawed fingers, long slim legs with three large, clawed toes on each foot, and a very elongated, tapering tail. The tail would be a helpful counterbalance as *Compsognathus* ran and changed direction rapidly while chasing prey or escaping predators.

Diminutive Hunter

The excellent fossils of Solnhofen allow reconstruction of the area at the time of *Compsognathus*—the Late Jurassic Period, about 150 million years ago. A patchwork of low semidesert islands, bearing dry scrub and undergrowth and fringed by beaches and coral reefs, were separated by shallow salty lagoons at the edge of the Tethys Sea.

From its build and proportions, sharp teeth, large eyes, clawed fingers and long legs, *Compsognathus* is portrayed as a speedy, nimble pursuer of small prey, which might include insects, worms, and reptiles such as little lizards. Indeed, the German *Compsognathus* was preserved with the skeletal remains of a small lizard, *Bavarisaurus*, in the region of its chest and belly. This is interpreted as direct evidence that *Compsognathus* had just fed on this prey item, maybe swallowing it whole. The French specimen has similar but less distinct "last supper" evidence, suggesting consumption of lizards or similar reptiles. There is no evidence for a feathery body covering in *Compsognathus*. This may mean there was none or that it was not preserved; close relatives of this Jurassic mini-hunter are known to have some type of fuzzy, feather-like coat.

At the time of *Compsognathus*, the landmass that would become southern Europe consisted of arid islands on the Tethys Sea. Fossil locations suggest *Compsognathus*'s Late Jurassic range.

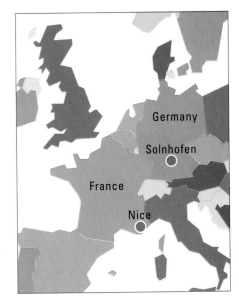

Miniature Sprinter

Modern sprinters, like this greyhound dog, have builds similar to *Lesothosaurus*, like elongated feet and shins. Similar bone structures likely indicate similar functions.

Lesotho is a smallish nation in southwest Africa, embedded within the Republic of South Africa. It was the site of fossil finds in the 1970s, named by Peter Galton in 1978 as *Lesothosaurus*, "Lesotho lizard" (see also *Fabrosaurus*). With a length of about 3 feet (1 m), this is one of the smallest known nonavian dinosaurs, but it belongs to a very different group than does *Compsognathus*, which was a saurischian (lizard-hipped). The remains of *Lesothosaurus* place it in the other major dinosaur grouping, the Ornithischia, or bird-hipped dinosaurs.

Lesothosaurus is significant because of its age, with fossils dating to the Early Jurassic Period 200–190 million years ago, and also because of its primitive or "old-fashioned" features. These give clues to the origins, early evolution, and spread of the whole Ornithischia group, a topic covered in Chapter 8.

Light and Speedy

Lesothosaurus fossils suggest that this herbivore was lightly built, although weight estimates vary from 8 to 22 pounds (3.6–10 kg). Its body shape and form, especially the relative lengths of the leg parts, indicate that it was a fast mover. The shin was longer than the thigh, and the foot and toes were also elongated. These are the proportions seen in rapid sprinting and running animals today.

Lesothosaurus has a small flattish head and short snout, with smooth upper front teeth and ridged "arrowhead" cheek teeth set slightly inward along the jaw, toward the midline. This may indicate that *Lesothosaurus* possessed fleshy cheeks that held plant food while it was chopped before swallowing. There is also the suggestion of a toothless, beak-like tip to the lower jaw. The small forelimbs ended in five-fingered hands. The main body may have been roomy enough for a considerable digestive tract, which would be necessary for breaking down plant food.

The Early Jurassic habitat of *Lesothosaurus* was probably dry and scrubby (see *Heterodontosaurus*, described on the next page). *Lesothosaurus* may have reared up or stooped to crop soft, low-growing vegetation, perhaps supporting some of its weight on its front limbs or using its fingers to scrape for small food items. If danger threatened, it could swing its body almost to a horizontal line and race away.

At one location, two *Lesothosaurus* fossils were in curled positions and worn teeth were also found. One interpretation is that the

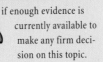

Leaf-shaped teeth suggest that *Lesothosaurus* chopped or shredded its food rather than grinding it; as an herbivore, it would use its speed to evade predators rather than catch prey.

small dinosaurs were inactive, perhaps surviving inhospitable conditions (such as a dry season), and their jaws had shed the worn teeth as replacement teeth grew.

Types of Teeth

Around the same place and time as *Lesothosaurus*—southern Africa in the Early Jurassic—lived another small plant-eating ornithischian dinosaur. This was *Heterodontosaurus*, "different/mixed-toothed lizard." It was certainly small, up to 4 feet (1.2 m), and weighing as little as 6 pounds (2.7 kg) according to some estimates, but as much as 22 pounds (10 kg) in others. *Heterodontosaurus* fossils were collected during a British-South African expedition in the early 1960s, led by teams from London's Natural History Museum and the University of London. The dinosaur was described and named in 1962 by Alfred Crompton and Alan Charig. Its closest relatives are ornithopods, the group that much later came to include massive herbivores such as *Iguanodon*.

Biting and Chewing

Most dinosaurs, and indeed most reptiles, have only one main design of tooth in the jaw. The teeth vary in size as they grow and are replaced, but they are all of the same shape. In the short, deep skull and jaws of *Heterodontosaurus* were set three distinctive types of teeth. At the front of the upper jaw, small sharp incisorlike teeth bit down onto the toothless predentary bone that tipped the lower jaw. Just behind were four long, fanglike, canine-type teeth, one pair in each jaw.

The strange, varied teeth of *Heterodontosaurus* ("different/mixed-tooth lizard") gave the dinosaur its name. The purpose of its unique dental design is unknown.

Each tooth fitted into a groove in the opposing jaw when the mouth closed. Toward the rear of the jaw were high-crowned, close-packed, ridged teeth, similar to modern molars.

The unique dentition of *Heterodontosaurus* has generated many suggestions as to their purpose. The small upper front teeth seem suited to biting, snipping, and nibbling, perhaps when gathering plant food. The rear teeth were probably used for crushing and chewing, and their position in the jaw suggests that *Heterodontosaurus* had fleshy cheeks to retain food during this process. Tooth-wear patterns and the jaw and skull structure suggest that *Heterodontosaurus* could chew with a side-to-side motion as well as the usual up-and-down movements.

Canine Puzzle

The functions of the larger tusklike canine teeth are less clear. Perhaps they were used to rip up larger, tougher food items. With their sharp edges, they could have been very helpful in self-defense, when the dinosaur might slash at enemies. A very different idea, based on the use of similar teeth among certain mammals such as musk deer, is that they served some kind of display purpose. They do not seem to occur in all of the fossil *Heterodontosaurus* specimens. Possibly they were possessed by one sex, perhaps the males, and used in visual displays or even physical combat against rival males at breeding time or to impress potential mates.

The hands of *Heterodontosaurus* were also distinctive. Each sported five fingers in two groups: the first three were longer and stronger, while the fourth and fifth (pinky) were much smaller. The overall hand design indicates that it was mobile and grasping. *Heterodontosaurus* may have grabbed vegetation stems or scrabbled in the dry soil of the time, digging for plant parts such as soft roots or juicy runners.

SPECIFICATIONS

Dinosaur: *Heterodontosaurus*
Meaning: Different-toothed Lizard
Order: Ornithischia
Family: Heterodontosauridae
Period: Early Jurassic
Size: 50 inches (1.3 m) long, 42 pounds (19 kg)
First discovered: South Africa by Dr. Alan Charig and Dr. Barry Cox while on expedition
Region: South Africa
Characteristics:
- Three different types of teeth: sharp upper front teeth, high-crowned cheek teeth, and two pairs of long canine tusks (possibly only in males), plus a horny beak for crushing, grinding, and chewing its food. May have also stored food in pouches within the mouth
- Five-fingered hands with sharp claws
- Bipedal but occasionally walked on all fours
- Hind legs were longer than the front, with three-toed feet and a long tail

New Contenders

In recent years, new discoveries have revised many ideas about very small nonavian dinosaurs—not only their sizes, but also their habits, and the relationships of various groups of dinosaurs to one another. For example, the not-quite-fully-grown, 4-foot (1.2 m) *Yinlong* ("hidden dragon") has affected understanding of the ceratopsians, or horned dinosaurs. This group contains mainly hulking, four-footed, Late Cretaceous herbivores such as *Triceratops*. *Yinlong* has the diagnostic rostral bone at the front of the upper jaw, which is not found in other dinosaurs (or other animals). Its fossils date back to the Late Jurassic Period, about 160–155 million years ago. This small reptile could walk on its two rear legs and suggests how the whole ceratopsian group might have originated.

Yinlong was named in 2006 from fossils located in Wucaiwan, in China's Xingjian province. It shows features also found in the pachycephalosaurs or "bonehead" dinosaurs,

Many recent finds in China have revealed tiny dinosaurs, some of which are only about 1 foot (30.5 cm) in length.

Wucaiwan

China

SMALLEST?

Smallness can come not only from genus or species, but also from youth. Fossil skeletons just 8 inches (20 cm) in length, the smallest of all known (nonavian) dinosaur skeletons, represent infants of *Mussaurus*, "mouse reptile." This early dinosaur, dating to the Late Triassic Period some 215–210 million years ago, lived in what is now Santa Cruz, Argentina, and was named in 1979. It was probably of the group known as prosauropods, which included *Plateosaurus*. Had the tiny *Mussaurus* specimens lived, they would have grown into adults about 10–13 feet (3–4 m) long, weighing perhaps 250–300 pounds (110–136 kg).

providing strong evidence that these two groups were related within the larger grouping known as the Marginocephalia ("shelf-heads"). *Yinlong* even has some similarities to heterodontosaurs such as *Heterodontosaurus*, indicating these may have been closely linked to the marginocephalians.

Eocursor

Going back further, to the Late Triassic Period some 210 million years ago, the "dawn runner" *Eocursor* offers an insight into the early stages of one of the two major dinosaur groups—the ornithischians or "bird-hips." Fossils of *Eocursor* come from the Karroo region

near Ladybrand, in South Africa's Free State. They were recovered in 1993 but not described and named until 2007. The remains include portions of most body parts, including the skull, backbone, front and rear limbs, and pelvis (hip bone). They show a plant-eater about 3 feet (almost 1 meter) long, with leaf-shaped teeth, strong grasping hands, and long rear legs indicating a bipedal gait.

Smaller Still

In the twenty-first century, more tiny dinosaurs continue to be discovered, especially in China. Some specimens of *Microraptor* ("small or tiny thief/ hunter/raider") were perhaps just 2 feet (60 cm) from nose to tail. (See chapter 4 for a fuller description of *Microraptor*, especially with respect to feathers and flight.)

Limited remains of a dinosaur known as *Parvicursor* ("small runner") found in the Late Cretaceous sediments near Khulsan, Mongolia, suggest an overall length in some estimates of just 20 inches (50 cm), although other approximations are twice this. Named in 1996, its fossils are incomplete— mainly rear legs and the hip region plus some vertebrae. *Parvicursor* was probably a kind of alvarezsaur, in the same group as *Shuvuuia*.

One of the smallest extinct dinosaurs ever found, remains of feathers can clearly be seen in this delicate, diminutive *Microraptor gui* from the Early Cretaceous.

CHAPTER 4

ANATOMICAL EXTREMES

SURVEYING THE ANIMAL WORLD TODAY, various extreme body structures catch the eye: the massively elongated trunk of the elephant; the huge spreading antlers of the male moose; the enormously lengthy neck of the giraffe; the fearsome front claws of the giant anteater; the great canine teeth of the hippopotamus. Some of these extraordinary pieces of anatomy have obvious physical uses. The elephant's multipurpose trunk can gather food, suck in water to be squirted into the mouth for drinking, discern odors with amazing sensitivity, and caress fellow herd members during social interactions. Other functions are less tangible, as when the male moose employs its antlers for intimidating rival males during the rut and for impressing females as potential mates.

Unlike these extant creatures, Mesozoic dinosaurs and their behavior cannot be observed. Thus it is not possible to confirm, or even propose, all the functions of their sometimes bizarrely exaggerated body parts and organs—which, in any case, are only known from limited skeletal remains. However, extrapolations from the living can be made for the dead, allowing scientists to speculate how and why dinosaur bodily features became greatly narrowed, stretched, widened, strengthened, or exaggerated in so many ways.

Dating back to 159–144 million years ago, *Archaeopteryx* (left) is widely regarded as the earliest bird in existence and was similar in size to the modern magpie (right).

The great sauropod dinosaurs described earlier are famed for supporting the longest necks of any creature. What advantages did this body feature confer in the habitat and conditions of their time?

Mamenchisaurus ("Mamenchi lizard"), discovered in 1952, was named after the watercourse at its fossil discovery site in Sichuan, China. Remains have also been found in Gansu and Xinjiang provinces. Most are dated as Late Jurassic, about 150–140 million years ago. In the first-unearthed remains the neck length was estimated to be 33–36 feet (10–11 m), for a total snout-to-tail-tip length of some 76 feet (22 m), and a body weight up to 20 tons. More recent finds of *Mamenchisaurus* hint at maybe 46 feet (14 m) of neck. In both these examples the neck would be around half the total length of the creature. At 19, the number of cervical vertebrae for *Mamenchisaurus* is extreme. This number varied in sauropods, but most living

If they held their necks relatively horizontally, Diplodocus and related sauropods could have used their long, heavy tail as a counterbalance.

SAVING WEIGHT

Many sauropod cervical vertebrae show weight-saving adaptations. The vertebrae have scoops and hollows that reduce the amounts of bone and also make room for muscles and tendons. Some have cavities or chambers that may have been filled in life with air, as in bird bones. Projections or rods of bone overlap and align the vertebrae to strengthen the neck structure, but at the expense of flexibility.

mammals, from giraffes to humans, have only seven.

Mostly Neck

Another great-necked sauropod was *Barosaurus* ("heavy lizard"), a North American Late Jurassic cousin of *Diplodocus*. Of a total length of up to 85 feet (26 m), the head and neck extended 30 feet (9 m) beyond the shoulders.

Another long-neck was discovered in the Gobi Desert in 2006. The Early

Cretaceous, titanosaurlike *Erketu* was named after a mighty deity from Mongolian tradition. Limited fossils allow only a provisional estimate of neck length at about 24 feet (7 m). But in terms of proportions, the study suggests that the neck could have been almost twice as long as the body.

Why So Long?

Sauropods are often depicted craning high into trees, the neck held in a graceful curve as the dinosaur browses elegantly. Some researchers now question these portrayals. Biomechanical calculations show that the power to pump blood so high would require a huge heart. It might beat so slowly that blood would drain back down before the next upsurge. A faster heartbeat would need the type of metabolism more associated with "warm-blooded" creatures, rather than the "cold-bloodedness" popularly associated with reptiles. As the head swung up and down, the high pressures involved could easily rupture tiny blood vessels and microscopic cells, especially in the brain, while the low pressures would mean

A similar shape may be a clue to similar behavior; thus, despite its much greater size, some scientists believe that *Brachiosaurus* acted much like a giraffe in using its height to reach food at the tops of trees.

that the dinosaur would have suffered blackouts.

Did these dinosaurs have various check valve systems in the neck arteries to reduce pressure and stop backflow or some other system? Impossible to say. Some scientists conclude that they did not lift their heads very high—perhaps no higher than the hump of the back. The relatively stiff neck could swing from side to side, bending near its base, in a great feeding arc as the dinosaur plodded forward. Or it may have reached out for plants over swampy ground or water, as the herbivorous version of a fishing pole, while the feet remained on the firm earth of the bank.

Skulls and Frills

One of the largest-ever land animal heads belonged to the herbivorous dinosaur *Torosaurus*. Its skull measured more than 7 feet (2.1 m) in length. More than a century ago, in 1891, the "bull/perforated lizard" *Torosaurus* was named by Othniel Charles Marsh. *Torosaurus* fossils were discovered by energetic U.S. fossil-finder John Bell Hatcher (1861–1904) in Niobrara county, Wyoming. Most of the preserved material is partial and skull-based, but there are also finds of the shoulder bones, forelimbs, and ribs.

Torosaurus was a Late Cretaceous ceratopsian ("horn-face") or horned dinosaur—a beaked plant-eater in the same group as well-known *Triceratops*. Its length was estimated at up to 26 feet (8 m) and 5 or 6 tons in weight. Like *Triceratops*, *Torosaurus* had one smaller nose horn and two long brow horns.

The head and frill of *Torosaurus* may seem huge. But an even larger rear-frilled skull was possessed by another Late Cretaceous ceratopsian from New Mexico and Colorado, *Pentaceratops*. One skull specimen measures almost 10 feet (3 m), the biggest known for any land-dweller.

Old Ideas

More than a dozen main kinds of ceratopsians with large neck frills are known, mostly from Late Cretaceous North America. Many also have long face horns, usually one on the nose and one above each eye. In addition, some of the frills have extra bony elements, known as epoccipitals, around their edges or margins. In *Styracosaurus* these were shaped like spikes or horns, increasing in length toward the top midline of the frill. In *Centrosaurus* the epoccipitals were rounded, forming a scalloped fringe, with longer curved hooked versions at the frill's top.

What were the purposes of such large and elaborate structures? An early suggestion, based on the heavy, solid frill of *Triceratops*, was self defense; perhaps *Triceratops* used the frill as a shield to protect his forequarters from attack. But in other ceratopsians the frill is not a curving sheet of solid bone. It has large openings or windows framed by strutlike bony members. This design would provide little protection against enemies. Another proposal cites the frill as an anchorage surface or housing for powerful jaw-moving muscles. However, the frill's extreme flaring proportions and lightweight build, and the pull lines of the muscles, make such a function extremely unlikely.

Visual Display

One line of current thinking sees the ceratopsian neck frill, along with the nose horns, as visual identification and display devices. In life, the frill's scaly skin covering may have been brightly colored and patterned. The dinosaur may have swung and tilted its head to show off the huge frill area and intimidating nose horns to greatest effect. One purpose of this display could be to identify its own kind and distinguish other kinds of ceratopsians, maybe when herding or breeding. Other aims might have been to intimidate rivals of the same sex at breeding time and to court potential mates. Also, a strikingly colored frill, coupled with fearsome horns, would make the dinosaur seem bigger and fiercer to possible predators and other enemies.

Further suggestions include flushing the frill skin with blood so that it changed color at certain times or even some kind of more elaborate cell-based color change system, as found in living reptiles such as chameleon lizards. Chameleons often change color to indicate their "mood" and intentions to mates, territorial rivals, or enemies, not just for simple camouflage. Perhaps this also occurred in the long-gone "horn-faced" reptiles.

Even frills with holes in them, if covered with skin, could appear impressive, and make *Anchiceratops* seem larger and fiercer.

Strange Heads

The basic design of the "original" dinosaur skull probably included a long tapering snout with tooth-equipped jaws, smooth forehead, eyes set on the sides of the head, and smallish braincase. But as the dinosaur group spread and diversified, this form became embellished in many ways. The Early Jurassic

out the remains to a University of California–Berkeley team. One very worn and two partial skeletons were studied by U.S. paleontologist Samuel Welles (1897–1997). In 1954, they were identified, like many larger Jurassic meat-eaters of the time, as a species of *Megalosaurus*.

The age of the rocks raised suspicions in Welles. He returned to the site—and found another, much better preserved specimen. This showed the strange feature of the twin curving ridges on the skull. Going back to the original specimens, Welles saw that the ridges had been on the earlier find, but they were crushed and distorted out of place into the cheek area. Welles recognized that this was no *Megalosaurus*; in 1970, he redescribed and renamed the dinosaur *Dilophosaurus*. It is usually included with early dinosaurs such as *Coelophysis* in the theropod group known as ceratosaurs.

The skull of *Dilophosaurus* bears two thin bony crests and an impressive array of teeth.

Period, 200–190 million years ago, saw one of the first sizeable theropods (bipedal meat-eaters) known from adequate remains. This was *Dilophosaurus* ("two-ridged/double-crested lizard"), named for the two curious bony crests on top of its head.

Dilophosaurus fossils were first excavated in 1942 from a Navajo reservation site near Tuba City, Arizona. Local Navajo Jesse Williams pointed

Symbol of Maturity

Dilophosaurus was probably about 20 feet (6 m) in length, with a weight of up to half a ton. It had sharp curved teeth, a sturdy neck, slim body, slender limbs with the rear pair being much larger, sharp hand and foot claws, and a long tapering tail. Overall, it had the form of an agile, light, but strong meat-eater.

The functions of the twin head crests have been much discussed. They are thin and fragile, and thus would have been of little use as weapons either for attack or defense. Their limited size seems to preclude any kind of thermo-regulation role in cooling or warming the body, as suggested for the large back "sails" of dinosaurs such as *Spinosaurus* or the back plates of stegosaurs.

Most proposals for the crests involve some kind of visual display, as previously mentioned for the neck frills of ceratopsian dinosaurs. Like a rooster's comb, the head crest could have been covered in colorful skin. It might have indicated the maturity, physical condition, and prowess of the owner. Simply displaying the crest might avert physical battles, for example, when rivals contested breeding rights or when disputing territorial occupation; another possibility is that the crest was used to impress

potential mates. Modern lizards engage in all of these behaviors.

Like its distant relative the rooster, *Dilophosaurus* may have had a brightly colored crest in order to impress rivals.

Mouths and Beaks

One of the most fascinating areas of dinosaur physiology is feeding mechanisms. The designs of dinosaur mouths and teeth can be related to animals of today, especially living birds and reptiles, to provide a wealth of clues about diet. Long, sharp, fanglike teeth indicate a meat-eater, and rows of ridged chopping or crush-ing rear teeth signify a her-bivore. But what about no teeth at all?

The Toothless Beak

The ornithomimosaurs ("bird mimic/imitator lizards") have the casual name of ostrich dinosaurs from their general body shape and proportions. They were mostly medium-sized, slim and lightly built, hollow-boned, long-necked, and long-limbed for fleet-footedness, with a bipedal gait—moving on the two rear legs. At the front end was a smallish, elongated, lightweight skull, very similar to a bird's in structure. It had large orbits, or eye sockets, presumably for big eyes that provided good vision. There were no teeth; the mouth was a long but light beaklike structure. In life this may have been covered by a horny, sharp-rimmed sheath, much as in a modern bird.

Two well-known ornithomimo-saurs from the Late Cretaceous are *Gallimimus* and *Ornithomimus*. Well-preserved fossils of the "chicken/fowl mimic" *Gallimimus*, officially named in 1972, are known from various localities

Except for feathers, *Gallimimus* may have appeared very similar to enlarged modern ostriches, and may have survived on a similar diet.

in the Gobi Desert. They represent a range of life stages, with adults reaching up to 20 feet (6 m) in length and weighing perhaps 900 pounds (410 kg). *Struthiomimus* ("ostrich mimic") is one of North America's best-known ornithomimosaurs. Smaller than *Gallimimus*, at up to 13 feet (4 m) and 330 pounds (150 kg), its remains come mainly from Alberta, Canada. This genus was named in 1917 by Henry Fairfield Osborn.

A *Struthiomimus* skeleton is poised to flee. Likely quite speedy, ostrich dinosaurs probably ran primarily to escape predators rather than to catch prey.

Feeding Strategies

The toothless, beaklike mouths of these and other ostrich dinosaurs have been interpreted as adaptations to an omnivorous diet—that is, consuming almost any type of food. No teeth means no chewing, so smaller items were swallowed whole and larger items might be pecked into smaller ones for gulping down. The ostrich of today can be called an omnivore, although it primarily consumes plant matter such as leaves, buds, fruits, and seeds, as well as small animals such as insects and lizards. As for the ostrich, the ornithomimosaur's long, flexible neck would allow adept pecking at edible items spotted by its large eyes.

More clues come from what might be interpreted as accessory feeding structures: the front limbs. In most ornithomimosaurs, these are relatively long with flexible joints and substantial claw-tipped fingers. In some, the fingers seem grouped to form a hook. Activities for these front limbs are variously suggested as scrabbling and digging for underground plant material, grubs, and bugs; snatching at small prey items such as lizards; or hooking vegetation such as leafy branches, fruits, and fronds toward the mouth.

The large number of ornithomimosaur fossils at some sites have been coupled with evidence of gastroliths, or "stomach stones." Associated with various dinosaurs, these pebbles were swallowed to help pulverize tough food in the digestive tract. These clues have led to suggestions that ornithomimosaurs were more herbivorous than carnivorous. Plant-eaters are more common in a habitat than meat-eaters, and internal milling would help ornithomimosaurs to digest demanding, low-nutrient vegetation.

Tiny—and Useless?

Vestiges, or vestigial body parts, are the remnants or traces of structures that presumably were once important and useful, but that have fallen into disuse and shrunken or faded into obscurity as a result of evolutionary change. An oft-cited example resides in the human body. This is the appendix (vermiform appendix), a finger-sized pouch branching from the start of the large intestine. It has seemingly no major function and only draws attention when it becomes inflamed, causing appendicitis.

Did some dinosaurs have vestigial bodily features? From fossil evidence, among the main contenders are the tiny, seemingly useless front limbs of great carnivores such as *Tyrannosaurus* and *Carnotaurus*.

Not so dainty: This *Tyrannosaurus rex* forearm, while small in comparison to the body, is nevertheless quite strong and ends in two fearsome claws.

Horned Bull

The "meat/flesh bull" *Carnotaurus* lived during the Late Cretaceous, in what is now the Chubut province of Argentine Patagonia. A fine skeleton, lacking only parts of the feet and tail, was studied and named in 1985 by eminent Argentinian paleontologist José Bonaparte (b. 1928). Even fossil skin impressions were available, showing nonoverlapping round scales, with larger scales, grading from low humps to taller cones, along the upper sides to the top of the back.

Carnotaurus was about 25 feet (7.6 m) long, around one ton in weight, and unusual for a theropod in many ways, especially in the shape and proportions of its head and face. The skull was deep and short, with a foreshortened snout and snub-nosed appearance reminiscent of a dinosaurian bulldog. Above each small eye jutted a bull-like horn, protruding sideways and slightly upward. Also extremely striking were the miniature forelimbs, seemingly out of any sensible proportion to the rest of the body. Each of these "dwarf arms" had a tiny hand with four minimal fingers. The skeletal proportions within the segments of the forelimb, being the upper arm, forearm, and wrist and hand, are also contradictory. The humerus, or upper arm bone, is sizeable and robust. Yet the ulna and radius in the forearm are ridiculously short, so that the hand seems attached to the elbow.

Forearmed, Forewarned

The diminutive forelimb proportions of *Carnotaurus* may be extreme. But various other theropods showed the same trend, not only *Tyrannosaurus* but also *Gorgosaurus*, *Albertosaurus*, and others. In *Tyrannosaurus*, the forelimbs were certainly small, almost the same length as an adult human arm. But they were well-built and strong, with two sharp-clawed fingers.

Ideas about the use of such tiny limbs are legion. They were too short to reach the mouth, or to cushion the dinosaur and prevent injury if it fell forward onto its chest while running. One suggestion was that the animal used them as aids when rising from lying or sitting position. An early proposal from Henry Fairfield Osborn was for the arms as grappling hooks or stabilizers to hold the partner when mating. Another hook theme is as meat hooks when feeding, to pull apart bits of carcass, as evidenced by the sharp claws.

Maybe the mini-arms had more than one function in some of these dinosaurs. But maybe in some the forelimbs were simply degenerating and drifting toward being vestigial.

From left to right, *Daspletosaurus*, *Tyrannosaurus rex*, and *Tarbosaurus* display the small arms typical of tyrannosaurs. Debate continues over the usage of these diminutive forelimbs.

Giant Claws

One of the strangest dinosaur groups was the therizinosaurs ("scythe lizards"). Knowledge of them stems from 1948, with the discovery of mysterious giant claws some 3 feet (1 m) long in Mongolia. They were given the name *Therizinosaurus* in 1954. Then came another claw find associated with a curious mix of other parts: limb remnants, with the front limb resembling the theropod pattern of predatory dinosaurs; a pelvis and four-toed foot more similar to the long-necked sauropod design; and a tooth reminiscent of a plant-eater. With such a strange combination of features, the mystery deepened.

Intriguing Features

From the 1970s, further finds, mainly Late Cretaceous from Mongolia and China, have provided new information on these extremely weird dinosaurs. They were within the theropod, or meat-eating, group and had similarities with the mani-

A therizinosaur, *Erlikosaurus* possessed enormous claws, the largest of which was as long as a human forelimb. It is presumed to have been an herbivore, using its claws to snatch vegetation, though some theorize that it may have used the claws for carnivorous purposes, like digging up insects or spearing small mammals.

GIANT FORELIMBS

One of the most enigmatic dinosaur fossils is *Deinocheirus* ("terrible hand"). The remains consist only of forelimb parts and possible bits of ribs and vertebrae. The forelimbs are an astonishing 8 feet (2.6 m) long. Each hand sports three robust claws about 10 inches (25 cm) in length. The Late Cretaceous fossils were uncovered in Mongolia's Nemegt region and named in 1970. Comparison of these scant remains to established dinosaur groups shows similarities to ornithomimosaurs, or ostrich dinosaurs, and perhaps maniraptorans. Scaling up the proportions, *Deinocheirus* could have been an ornithomimosaur some 33 feet (10 m) long, with a weight of 2 to 3 tons—by far the largest known ostrich dinosaur.

raptorans such as *Deinonychus* from which birds evolved. But their general form seemed bulky and clumsy, with a plant-cropping beak, weak plant-chopping cheek teeth, long neck, tubby body, short strong legs, an upright bipedal posture, short tail, and extraordinary forelimbs with each hand bearing three outsize claws.

Suggested claw uses range from hooking plant material toward the mouth through self-defense to some kind of intimidating display when breeding, and even (from a giant anteater analogy) digging for small, soft

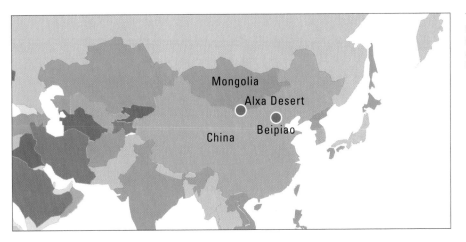

Therizinosaur fossils have been found in Mongolia, China, and North America, and are dated to the Cretaceous Period.

food items such as termites. However, how such a large creature might have existed on such minuscule food items is difficult to explain.

Scythe Profiles

One of the better-known therizinosaurs is *Erlikosaurus*. Named in 1980 to honor the demon of the dead in Mongolian tradition, it was probably some 20 feet (6 m) long and weighed around 350 to 400 pounds (160–180 kg). Particularly valuable was the skull, absent in most other therizinosaur finds. It showed a long, toothless, birdlike beak at the front and small rear teeth, shaped like leaves, suited to chopping plant food.

Alxasaurus fossils, recovered from Mongolia's Alxa (Alashan) Desert and named in 1993, came from the Early Cretaceous, about 115–100 million years ago. In some ways they represent a transitional stage between a theropod meat-eater and the later, more highly evolved therizinosaur herbivores. *Alxasaurus* measured about 13 feet (4 m) in length.

Beipiaosaurus, named in 1999 for the Chinese city of Beipiao near where its fossils were found, dates from an earlier time, 125–120 million years ago. It was some 7 feet (2.1 m) long and weighed about 180 pounds (80 kg). An exciting find was filamentlike structures that could have covered its forelimbs and perhaps other body surfaces. This has led to the speculation that some therizinosaurs were "feathered."

Extrapolating information from these more recent discoveries suggests that the original find, *Therizinosaurus*, might have reached a massive 39 feet (12 m) in length and weighed an ungainly 5 tons.

Ancient Wing

Some of the world's best known, most precious, and most beautiful fossils are of *Archaeopteryx* ("ancient wing"). The first remains of this creature were uncovered some 150 years ago and, despite exciting recent finds, it is still the earliest known bird.

Only 10 or so *Archaeopteryx* specimens have been identified, all from the Solnhofen region of Bavaria, southern Germany; all date to the Late Jurassic Period, around 155–150 million years ago. One specimen was originally considered to be a pterosaur, while another was first thought to be a small meat-eating dinosaur such as *Compsognathus*, whose remains come from the same time and place.

Aptly named "ancient wing," *Archaeopteryx* possessed feathers fully adapted for flight.

As described earlier, the region in the Late Jurassic was a montage of flattish islands, coral reefs, and shallow, salty lagoons. The climate was warm but semiarid, supporting limited tree growth and dry scrub rather than lush forest.

Solnhofen Treasures

The very fine-grained limestones formed from the lagoon beds have preserved exquisite details in the fossils. The stone is called "lithographic," having once been quarried around Solnhofen for use in printing. The first examples of *Archaeopteryx* were described and named by German paleontologist Hermann von Meyer (1801–69) in 1861 and 1862. This was just a couple of years after the publication of *On the Origin of Species*, the epochal book by English naturalist Charles Darwin (1809–82) that proposed the theory of evolution by natural selection.

Archaeopteryx has since figured heavily in evolutionary discussions. The most recently publicized *Archaeopteryx* fossil, scientifically described in 2005, is one of the most complete. Known as the Thermopolis specimen, it was for many years held privately by a Swiss collector. It is now under the care of the Wyoming Dinosaur Center.

Mosaic of Features

Archaeopteryx fossils are among the most intensively studied and extensively debated in all of paleontology. Broadly, the creature shows a mosaic, or patchwork, of features from maniraptoran theropod dinosaurs, the meat-eating group to which *Deinonychus* and other "raptors" belong, and features from modern birds. (Maniraptorans, and how birds and flight may have evolved from them, are described on the following pages.)

Archaeopteryx was about 20 to 24 inches (50–60 cm) in length. It had the traditional predatory dinosaurian features of teeth in its jaws, a long bony tail, clawed fingers on its forelimbs, a flattish sternum (breastbone), and gastralia, often called "belly ribs." No modern flying birds show any of these features.

First Known Flier

Archaeopteryx's wing feathers seem shaped for flight, with a stiff central shaft supporting a vane of barbs and barbules, as an asymmetric design. Feathers of various kinds were once assumed to be exclusive to birds, but they are now known to have occurred in numerous theropod dinosaurs. *Archaeopteryx* also showed forelimbs modified as wings for flight; it had a bone in the upper chest (the furcula) formed from robust, fused clavicles (collar bones). The furcula is familiar in modern birds as the "wishbone," and a range of nonavian theropod dinosaurs also displayed this feature. Overall, some features of *Archaeopteryx*, once believed to be exclusive to birds, are now known from many nonavian theropods.

Numerous analyses of *Archaeopteryx*'s aerial prowess, looking at feather dynamics, skeletal form, and projected muscle layout, suggest that it could fly in a sustained and controlled fashion. However, it would not have been as strong and aerobatic as most birds today.

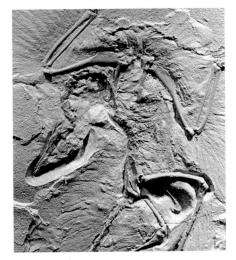

Impressions of feathers can be seen fanning out from this fossilized *Archaeopteryx*, the earliest known bird.

Feathers and Beaks

Recent fossil finds in East Asia, particularly China, have led to the reshaping of traditional concepts about dinosaurs and birds. In particular, varied views have been expressed about the functions of feathers and how flight evolved.

Caudipteryx ("tail feather") lived 130–125 million years ago in the Early Cretaceous. Its remains come from near Sihetun village, in China's northeast province of Liaoning. The first specimens were formally named in 1998 by Ji Qiang, Philip Currie, and colleagues. About the size of a turkey, at 3 feet (1 m) in length and 15 pounds (7 kg) in weight, *Caudipteryx* shows distinct feathers 6 inches (15 cm) or longer on its

tail, as well as feathers at the ends of its short forelimbs. The tail feathers may have been able to fan out, like a peacock's, for display purposes; the front limb feathers would not support flight. The rear limbs were long and strong, indicating a fast, adept mover, and the beaklike mouth had small, spiked upper front teeth. *Caudipteryx* is regarded by many authorities as a maniraptoran theropod, from the group that includes *Oviraptor*—that is, a nonavian dinosaur rather than a bird.

Microraptor ("small thief") was another feathered dinosaur from the same region and time span. A member of the raptor group, the dromaeosaurs, it was certainly tiny, with a total length of about 2 feet (60 cm). Six known specimens show distinct flight feathers, not only on the forelimbs, but also toward the ends of the hind limbs, in addition to a feather-fringed tail.

More Liaoning Wonders

Sinosauropteryx ("Chinese lizard wing/feather") was the first feathered dinosaur from the Liaoning deposits to be named, in

Two *Confuciusornis* birds would not appear out of place among a flock of modern hawks. They share features of today's birds and their nonavian theropod cousins.

1996. It is usually regarded as a theropod, but not as a dromaeosaur or oviraptorosaur, some of whose members are known to be feathered. It has been included with the tiny hunter *Compsognathus*, which extends feathering into a new dinosaur group.

The long tail feathers of ancient theropods like *Caudipteryx* and *Confuciusornis* may have fanned out like a modern peacock's, and served a similar display purpose.

Sinosauropteryx was up to 4 feet (1.2 m) long, of which most was its extremely long tail, and weighed perhaps 4 to 6 pounds (2–3 kg). Highly debated are possible nonflight "proto-feathers," which are simple two-branched fiber- or filamentlike structures, some more than 1 inch (2.5 cm) long. They may have been feathery, downy plumes, or even preserved frill-like fibers of the skin protein collagen.

Yet another Early Cretaceous (125–120 million years ago) creature from Liaoning, *Confuciusornis*, was named "Confucius bird" in 1995, in honor of the ancient Chinese philosopher. This early bird is known from many fossils of adults and juveniles. It had a head-to-tail length, excluding feathers, of about 10 to 12 inches (25–30 cm). It possessed features not seen in flying birds today, such as three clawed fingers at the leading edge of each wing, and a flattish sternum (breastbone) without the flange-shaped keel to anchor powerful wing-flapping muscles. Nevertheless, its wings have feathers and are designed for flight.

Some *Confuciusornis* specimens show structures, streaming out at the rear end, that can be interpreted as long, trailing tail feathers. These individuals may have been from one sex, using their tails for display when breeding, while the other sex lacked them. The horny beak was toothless (unlike *Archaeopteryx*), a feature that would not crop up in other bird groups until many millions of years later.

Flying Dinosaurs

Many thousands of dinosaur species are known to fly—they are the birds alive today. This may seem to be a strange statement. As a comparison, consider another group that has mastered the air: bats. These are furry, feed their young on milk, and show many other features that make them mammals, having descended from more "typical" mammalian ancestors. But bats also have their own distinctive characteristics, such as forelimbs highly modified into flight wings. Similarly, birds have their distinctive features, but they descended from dinosaurs. So, as bats are mammals, birds are dinosaurs.

This African fish eagle, like all birds from penguins to sparrows, is actually a dinosaur. Birds are the only remnants of the mighty rulers of the Mesozoic.

Twist of the Wrist

The dinosaurs usually identified as giving rise to birds were the theropods known as maniraptorans, "hand snatchers." This refers to a particular type of wrist structure that incorporated a half-moon-shaped wrist bone—the semilunate carpal block. Along with the typical maniraptoran elongated arm and hand, the wrist joint allowed a twisting or swiveling motion. Its original function may have been to grasp or grab, perhaps at prey. But it was also suited or preadapted to the particular flapping-twisting arm-hand motion involved in flight.

Maniraptorans share other features, too, including the furcula, or wishbone, in the upper chest. The group includes the dromaeosaurs or "raptors" such as *Velociraptor* and *Deinonychus*, the *Oviraptor* group, the strange therizinosaurs such as *Beipiaosaurus*, and, of course, birds.

Feather Types

Flight requires wings; in birds, the wing surfaces are provided by feathers. Once, feathers were seen as a defining avian feature: any animal with them was a bird. But recent fossil discoveries, especially in China (see previous pages), have yielded a whole array of nonbird dinosaurs with varying kinds of feathers and feather-like structures. These vary from simple fibers, strands, or fluffy down, popularly termed "dino-fuzz," to feathers much more like those of birds.

Some of these feather types were obviously unsuited to flight. What were they for? One suggestion is visual display to rivals or potential mates at breeding time. Another is camouflage. Or forelimb feathers may have formed a kind of "net" or "basket" for capturing prey with a wrist-twisting grab action. A further idea is that downy or hairy types of coverings provided insulation to retain body warmth during cold conditions. This, along with other lines of evidence, implies these dinosaurs were "warm-blooded," as discussed in chapter 7.

Up or Down?

How did early kinds of feathers lead to true flight? There are several proposals. The cursorial or "ground-up" version says that small dinosaurs, already equipped with forelimb feathers, took to holding out and flapping their arms as they ran, perhaps to gain speed. Gradually they ran less and flapped more. In the arboreal, or "tree-down," suggestion, the dinosaurs would have been adept climbers. They began to use their feathered forelimbs as gliding surfaces to swoop downward. Gradually improved flapping turned glides into powered flight.

Yet another idea is "tree-tree." Analysis of *Microraptor* indicates that it probably swooped from tree to tree with its forelimb wings held higher than its hind limb wings, in a "staggered biplane" configuration. It is not clear if this four-winged, or tetrapteryx, stage was an experimental sideline that left no legacy. Alternatively, it was a stage in the evolution of bird flight that was superseded when the rear limbs lost their involvement, leaving only the forelimb wings.

Going up? Whether dinosaurs took off, hopped down, or swooped from tree to tree, scientists agree that birds are the last living dinosaurs.

CHAPTER 5

FIRST AND LAST

FROM KNOWN FOSSIL FINDS, dinosaurs were present on Earth about 228–227 million years ago, at the start of the Late Triassic Period. Those early dinosaurs, including *Herrerasaurus* and *Eoraptor*, were mostly bipedal carnivores; that is, they had a two-legged gait and ate mainly other animals. Dinosaurs from before this time, around 230 million years ago, did not leave much fossil evidence.

Leap forward about 165 million years, through a vast span of dinosaur domination, and the last of the nonavian dinosaurs roamed the land. It was just before the end-of-Cretaceous mass extinction that saw the whole dinosaur group perish, along with many other kinds of animals on the land, in the air, and in the waters, plus numerous plant types. Like the early dinosaurs, some of those late representatives were still bipedal carnivores, such as the mighty *Tyrannosaurus*. But other, extremely diverse forms showed how varied the group had become. These late arrivals included many herbivores, such as the ceratopsians or "horn-faces" like *Triceratops*; the curious pachycephalosaurs, nicknamed "dome-heads" from the thickened bone of the skull roof; and the hadrosaurs, often called "duckbills" because of the shape of the front of the mouth, which was flattened, toothless, and beaklike.

Hadrosaur herds wander across the warm Cretaceous landscape. During this period, flowering plants made their first appearance, a development which may have suited the herbivorous hadrosaurids quite well.

Origins of Dinosaurs

To trace the evolutionary origins of the Dinosauria, it helps to track back through time and look at the various groups that, one after another, may have led to the first dinosaurs.

Eggs and Heads

A convenient starting place for tracing dinosaur origins is the group known as the Amniota. Its defining feature is the amniotic egg, which has a fluid-filled sac around the embryo. This attribute freed the female from laying eggs in water or moist places, as modern amphibians must do. Thus, amniotes could spread to drier areas. From indirect fossil evidence, the amniotic egg probably arose during the Carboniferous Period. Amniotes include the traditional groupings of reptiles, birds, and mammals.

The next feature to examine on the way to dinosaurs are holes in the head. More accurately, they are temporal fenestrae, gaps or "windows" on the sides of the skull. There are three basic patterns. Anapsids have no such openings, and include turtles and tortoises. Synapsids have one window on each side, usually just behind the eye socket. A well-known example was the sail-backed carnivore *Dimetrodon*, a pelycosaur from the Permian "Red Beds" of Texas. Later some synapsids developed fur or hair and evolved into mammals.

The third group of amniotes is the diapsids, with two temporal fenestrae on each side of the skull. The preserved remains of diapsid skulls, teeth, hip, and ankle bones show that at some time during the Late Permian, the diapsids gave rise to two further groups: the lepidosaurs, which includes today's lizards and snakes, and the archosaurs, sometimes referred to as "ruling reptiles."

Archosaurs

An early archosaur was *Euparkeria*. It was close to 5 feet (1.4 m) in length, weighed around 40 pounds (18 kg), and lived in southern Africa in Early Triassic times. With scaly skin, sharp teeth, and rear legs larger than the front ones, for occasional bipedal running, at a quick glance a lifelike reconstruction could be mistaken for a dinosaur.

Modern turtles, which lay their amniotic eggs under sand for protection while they incubate, may provide clues to the egg-laying behavior of dinosaurs, which were also amniotes.

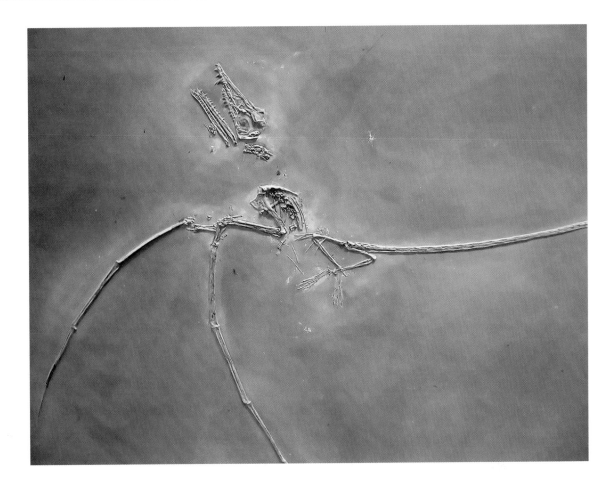

The archosaurs gave rise to two further groups. The crurotarsians/pseudosuchians included crocodilelike parasuchids, rauisuchians, and herbivorous aetosaurs, which all became extinct, and living crocodiles and alligators. The ornithodirans include *Marasuchus* and *Lagerpeton*. Both lived during the Middle Triassic in what is now Argentina. They were around 2 to 3 feet (0.6–0.9 m) in length, of slender build, with small sharp teeth, and hind limbs larger than front ones, again for running or jumping bipedally. All in all, they were not dissimilar to some early dinosaurs. Indeed, the ornithodirans probably went on to produce two groups with more familiar names: pterosaurs and dinosaurs.

Pterosaur fossils have been found virtually all over the world. The first vertebrate animals to achieve flight, some pterosaurs were also the largest animal fliers ever, with wingspans up to 40 feet (12 m).

Early Members?

Tracing evolutionary changes in ancient times from preserved remains is an extremely tricky process. The sparse, fragmentary nature of the fossil record and the various approaches to interpreting it may never provide an absolute answer to the question: What was the first dinosaur? To answer decisively would mean having to identify a particular point along an evolutionary sequence and regard every organism before it as nondinosaur and all that came after as dinosaurs.

and whether they were truly dinosaurs—perhaps they were some kind of precursor or even "sister" animals from contemporary evolutionary lines rather than the main dinosaur lineage.

Eoraptor

The "dawn thief/raider" *Eoraptor* is known from fossils found in northwest Argentina and dated to about 228 million years ago. In many ways, and considering the possible ancestors of dinosaurs as explained on the previous pages, it could resemble a prototype or early dinosaur.

Eoraptor was about 3 feet (1 m) in

Eoraptor's name is derived from the Greek word for dawn, *eo*, and the Latin word *raptor*, meaning thief or raider. It connotes *Eoraptor*'s status as one of the earliest known dinosaurs.

length and weighed perhaps 20 pounds (9 kg), although estimates are difficult to make because the main known specimen is a juvenile. Slimly built, it had hollow bones, a long snout, a longish neck, and an elongated, tapering tail. The teeth were small and mostly pointed, but not all of them had the classic curved, serrated or saw-edged design seen in later carnivorous dinosaurs. The rear limbs were long and slender, with three clawed toes

Several candidates from the first part of the Late Triassic Period, around 230–225 million years ago, present themselves for consideration as very early dinosaurs. But views differ on the status of these creatures

bearing the weight plus a dew claw higher up the foot. The front limbs were shorter and more armlike, and each hand was equipped with five grasping fingers, although two were much reduced.

The first remains of *Eoraptor*, a skull and most of a skeleton, were uncovered in 1991 by Ricardo Martinez. They come from rocks known as the Ischigualasto Formation, in northwestern Argentina. Remains of perhaps three individuals have now been excavated and the dinosaur was named by Paul Sereno and colleagues in 1993. It is seen as a saurischian, or lizard-hipped, dinosaur, and probably an early "primitive" or "basal" theropod, the group to which all bipedal meat-eating dinosaurs belong.

VALLEY OF THE MOON

The landscape in northwestern Argentina yielding remains of possible early dinosaurs such as *Eoraptor*, *Herrerasaurus*, and *Pisanosaurus* is dry and eroded today. From its bare craggy nature, it is known locally as the Valley of the Moon. The species name *Eoraptor lunensis*, "of the Moon," refers to this. But in the early Late Triassic, the region was an upland river valley where plants grew well in the wet season.

However, its five-fingered hands and varied tooth pattern are features that emphasize the "basal" part of this description. Other very early dinosaurs, *Herrerasaurus* and *Pisanosaurus*, are known from the same region and time, as described on the next pages.

The fossilized backbone and upper limbs of an *Eoraptor* emerge from the earth in Argentina's Valley of the Moon.

An Early Hunter

The name of the Andean goat-herding rancher and farmer Victorino Herrera lives in the annals of paleontology in the form of *Herrerasaurus*, an early dinosaur from the start of the Late Triassic Period, about 228 million years ago. Herrera first noticed its fossils in 1958–59, in the region of northwest Argentina known as the Valley of the Moon (see previous page). The rocks here, called the Ischigualasto Formation, are commemorated in the species part of the name, *Herrerasaurus ischigualastensis*. The first finds were fragmentary and were named in 1963 by Osvaldo Reig. But a fine complete skull and more pieces were located in 1988, allowing detailed study and analysis.

Herrerasaurus was an approximate contemporary of *Eoraptor*, described earlier. But it was a larger, stronger, more fearsome predator. With an overall length of some 10 feet (3 m), its weight estimates range from 80 pounds (36 kg) to more than double this. Based on other fragments, some authorities contend that this creature could have reached 15 feet (4.6 m) in length.

The snout of *Herrerasaurus* was elongated and tapering, and the jaws bristled with curved sharp teeth, much more typical of a predator than the teeth of *Eoraptor*. The rear legs were slim but powerful, with the relatively elongated shins and feet typical of a rapid mover. The arms were short and thin, but the hands had a strong grasping design. As in *Eoraptor*, the feet bore the weight on three larger clawed toes, with a smaller dew claw off the ground; the fourth and fifth digits of the five-fingered hand were much reduced. With its long bendable neck, slim body, and extremely slender tail forming half of the overall length, *Herrerasaurus* gives the impression of a fast, agile hunter.

A Strange Mixture

Herrerasaurus has some slightly more "advanced" or derived features in comparison to *Eoraptor*, but these are curiously mixed with early or "primitive" (basal) features—not all of them dinosaurian. A joint in the lower jaw allowed the front portion of the jaw to flex against the rear part, for a grab-grasp action when biting. The arms had proportions seen in much later theropods. The teeth are slim and blade-shaped, and they have the

Erosion in the Valley of the Moon reveals layers of geological rock, allowing scientists to accurately date fossilized remains embedded in the soil.

SPECIFICATIONS

Dinosaur: *Herrerasaurus*

Meaning: Herrera's reptile
Order: Saurischia
Family: Herrerasauridae
Period: Middle to Late Triassic
Size: 10 feet (3 m) long, 80–154 pounds (36–70 kg)
First discovered: 1958, San Juan, Argentina,
  by Victorino Herrera
Region: South America
Characteristics:
- Very long feet and toes to facilitate speed
- Small head
- Bipedal with short thighs and long feet
- Short forearms with five fingers on each hand
- Carnivore

serrations typical of later carnivores. More seemingly contradictory traits are seen in the sacral vertebrae at the base of the spinal column, the orientation of the hip bone, the acetabulum (socket in the hip bone for the ball-shaped end of the thigh bone), and the proportions of the fingers.

Broadly, *Herrerasaurus* possessed most but not all of the usual theropod features, perhaps apart from some hip and leg bone structures. But was it a theropod? Views on its grouping, and their implications for dinosaur origins, are included on the next page. (Remains of a smaller but similar animal, sometimes referred to as *Ischisaurus*, are actually from the genus *Herrerasaurus*.)

Much less debated is the diet of *Herrerasaurus*. Its size and strength suggest that it probably preyed on small-to-mid-sized animals. Suitable prey might have included the pig-sized, plant-munching reptiles known as rhynchosaurs, such as *Hyperodapedon*, and the vaguely crocodile-shaped, herbivorous aetosaurs such as *Stagonolepis*. Possible other meals included the early dinosaur *Pisanosaurus*, and cynodonts or mammal-like reptiles such as *Belesodon*.

Herrerasaurus hunts alone though the Triassic landscape. Few specifics can be surmised about its hunting methods, or even its diet.

Dinosaurs Get Going

The discovery of *Herrerasaurus*, described on the previous page, had various implications for dinosaur origins. This creature was at one time considered to be an archosaur, in a "sister" group to early dinosaurs, and not as a dinosaur itself. Others thought it to be an early but already oddly specialized dinosaur, with a mix of early and later traits. Eventually, the verdict became that it was an early saurischian, or lizard-hipped, dinosaur, and within the saurischians, a theropod—a bipedal, meat-eating dinosaur, albeit a very early or "basal" one.

single-origin group Dinosauria had already arisen, and then that this group had diverged into saurischians, or lizard-hips, and ornithischians, or bird-hips, and maybe the saurischians had also diverged into the bipedal, carnivorous theropods and the line leading to the long-necked, plant-gathering prosauropods and giant sauropods.

Finds during 1996–99 of fragmentary fossils in southwest Madagascar were suspected to be the early dinosaurian plant-eaters known as prosauropods, possibly even more ancient than *Herrerasaurus*. The

remains included jawbones of pony-sized animals. Further studies show that these may not have been actual dinosaurs, but more distant relations belonging to the general archosaur group. However, there remain three-toed fossil footprints from France that could have been made by theropod dinosaurs, and these date from the Middle Triassic, which could push dinosaur origins back to before 230 million years ago.

Archosaurs first evolved around 240 million years ago. Early relationships between various dinosaur species and archosaurs are often debated by scientists.

The determination that *Herrerasaurus* was a theropod implies that dinosaurs had been around for some time when the early predator arrived on the scene. It supposes that the

Pisanosaurus

Small, slim, and dainty, "Pisano's lizard" is known from one partial skeleton that was excavated, as with *Eoraptor* and *Herrerasaurus*, from Argentina's "Valley of the Moon" Ischigualasto Formation. It was named by Rodolfo Casamiquela in 1967 to honor his colleague Juan Pisano. About 3 feet (1 m) in length and weighing 8 pounds (3.6 kg), the remains suggest that *Pisanosaurus* was an ornithischian, or bird-hipped, dinosaur from about 228–221 million years ago. If so, it is one of the earliest known ornithischians.

Staurikosaurus

The fossils of "Southern Cross lizard" hail from southern Brazil's Santa Maria formation, Rio Grande do Sul, and were described and named in 1970 by Edwin Colbert. *Staurikosaurus* is known mainly from a spinal column, parts of the legs, and the lower jaw. It was probably about 7 feet (2 m) long. Because of its leg structure, jaw joint, and small, sharp, back-curved teeth, it is usually regarded as an early theropod, related to *Herrerasaurus*.

Chindesaurus

In 1984, Bryan Small recovered the remains of a theropod-type dinosaur from the famed Petrified Forest National Park in Arizona. The name

The three-toed footprint of a theropod from Enciso, Spain. Similar footprints dating back more than 230 million years may also have been made by theropods.

Chindesaurus was bestowed in 1995 from the discovery site of Chinde Point and the term *chindii*, Navajo for "ghost" or "spirit." The fossils date from the Late Triassic and suggest a slim bipedal carnivore with a length of up to 12 feet (almost 4 m).

Saltopus

Known from poorly preserved fossils found near Elgin, Scotland, *Saltopus* or "leaping foot" was only 2 or 3 feet (60–90 cm) long. It was probably an archosaur and perhaps an ornithodiran, but it is far from certain whether it was predinosaurian or a dinosaur. It seems to have been very slender in build.

Last of the Hunters

Tyrannosaurus is notable in many respects, especially as one of the largest meat-eaters ever to walk the Earth, as detailed earlier in this book. This huge hunter was also one of the last of the nonbird dinosaurs. Some of its remains have been dated to about 67 or 66 million years ago. This is almost nudging the time of the end-of-Cretaceous mass extinction, usually estimated at 65.5 million years ago.

Just as the famous specimen "Sue" shed light on the life and times of *Tyrannosaurus,* the discovery of the marvelous skeleton nicknamed "Stan" has revealed unique glimpses of the colossal carnivore's world. Like Sue, the skeleton's name comes from its discoverer, in this case, fossil enthusiast and part-time prospector Stan Sacrison. In 1987, he was searching the sandstone cliffs and crags near Buffalo in northwest South Dakota (Sue was found near the town of Faith in the same state).

The rocks here are known as the Hell Creek Formation and have yielded huge numbers of excellent dinosaurian and other fossils for well over a century.

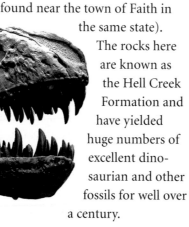

This skull of an adult *Tyrannosaurus rex* shows off the massive, serrated teeth, which would help the dinosaur saw the meat from its prey.

SPECIFICATIONS

Dinosaur: *Tyrannosaurus*
Meaning: Tyrant reptile
Order: Saurischia
Family: Tyrannosauridae
Period: Late Cretaceous
Size: 40 feet (12.4 m) long, 5–7 tons
First discovered: 1902, Hell Creek, Montana, United States, by Barnum Brown
Region: North America and Asia
Characteristics:
- Gigantic skull measured 4.5 feet long (1.4 m)
- Mouth held approximately 50 cone-shaped serrated teeth which could chew through bone and regrow when lost
- To compensate for its large cranium, the tail was equally massive and contained as many as 40 vertebrae
- Most of the skeletal build consisted of hollow bones
- Relatively small forearms with two small fingers on each

Stan (the man) noticed what seemed to be a pelvis, or hip bone, and set to work on its excavation. As the magnitude of the find became apparent, workers from the Black Hills Institute at Hill City, South Dakota, were called in. Some 30,000 hours of preparation finally yielded a magnificent *Tyrannosaurus* that was about two-thirds complete. Stan (the fossil) soon went on world tour with a traveling exhibition, being unveiled at its first stop in Tokyo, Japan, in 1995. When the tour concluded, fossil Stan returned to the Black Hills Institute as a permanent exhibit.

The World of Stan

Fossils excavated with Stan, and from numerous digs across the Hell Creek Formation over the years, help to paint a picture of the region when the Cretaceous Period drew to a close. In vivid contrast to the landscape today, it was a subtropical mosaic of rivers and lush vegetation. Low plant growth included ferns and horsetails, with tall stands of trees related to modern redwoods, ginkgoes (maidenhair trees), and palms. Stan was no vegetarian and must have preyed on dinosaurs, including duckbilled *Edmontosaurus*, horned *Triceratops*, and armored *Ankylosaurus*, perhaps picking off the young, old, weak, and ill. The ecology of the area also included lizards, crocodiles, pterosaurs, and small mammals.

In the Wars

Stan was probably about 20 years old at death. Vital statistics include almost 200 fossilized bones recovered, a total length of about 40 to 42 feet (12.2–12.8 m), an estimated weight of 5 to 6 tons, and up to 58 teeth in the almost perfectly preserved skull, which shows details of the slippage and hinge joints that allowed such a wide gape and powerful bite.

During its life, Stan may have suffered several sets of injuries; some interpret the bones as showing damage, regrowth, scarring, and healing. Some of these may have included a head wound and a fractured rib. *Tyrannosaurus* may have battled each other, although why they would have done so is far from clear.

While its offspring watches eagerly, a *Tyrannosaurus rex* brings down a juvenile *Hypacrosaurus*.

Three Horns, Big Frill

One of the last nonavian dinosaurs, a sturdy and bulky herbivore from Late Cretaceous North America, is also one of the most instantly recognizable. The name *Triceratops*, "three horned face," refers to the two very long facial horns, up to 3 feet (1 m), with one on each eyebrow region, and the shorter but still considerable nose horn. Fossils of this ceratopsian, or "horn-face," date from about 68 to 65 million years ago. They have been recovered from several provinces and states in North America, including Alberta and Saskatchewan, and south to Wyoming and Colorado.

Triceratops sported a relatively short but sweeping neck frill in addition to its horns. Unlike many of the frills of other ceratopsians, which had large gaps or "windows," that of *Triceratops* was constructed from solid bone, covering the back of the dinosaur's neck. As described on earlier pages, the functions of the face horns and neck frills in this group of dinosaurs are much discussed. Opinion has varied from some kind of self-defense to visual display purposes and perhaps ritualized horn-locking as the animals challenged rivals and/or attracted mates at breeding time.

A *Triceratops* skull. Some experts believe *Triceratops* typically lived in groups, as animals alone would be more vulnerable.

Biggest of the Group

Triceratops was the largest of the known ceratopsians. It reached a length of 30 feet (9 m) and weighed perhaps 8 tons. Its build was stocky and powerful, dominated by the facial horns and flaring neck frill. The rear legs were longer than the front, so the back sloped up toward the hips, while the relatively short, tapering tail sloped down to near the ground. Its toothless, horn-covered "beak" was suited to cropping low-growing plant material; the cheek teeth of the upper and lower jaws were arranged in batteries and moved past each other with a shearing action, as described on later pages.

Too Many Species

Fossils of *Triceratops* were first studied in the late 1880s (see panel), and the genus was named in 1889 by Othniel Charles Marsh. Over the following years many variations on the basic *Triceratops* theme were uncovered,

showing preserved individuals with slightly smaller, larger, or differently shaped frills, and assorted relative lengths of brow and nose horns. A naming frenzy ensued, so that at certain times the genus encompassed 12 or more individual species.

In the 1980s, a review by John Ostrom and Peter Wellnhofer concluded that all these variants were the result of differences in sex, age, maturity, and preservation conditions. They represented the natural variation of one species, *Triceratops horridus* ("roughened"), as originally named by Marsh. Further work suggests there may, in fact, be two species, *T. horridus* and *T. prorsus*, with possibly a separate genus, provisionally *Diceratops*, for the distinctive form once known as *T. hatcheri*.

A *Triceratops* skeleton on display at the Smithsonian Institution's National Museum of Natural History.

ALMOST A BUFFALO

The first remains of *Triceratops* came to light in 1887. They consisted of only a skull roof with the bony cores of two brow horns. Othniel Charles Marsh examined the find and concluded that it represented not a dinosaur from the end of the Cretaceous Period, but a long-horned bison from the Pliocene Epoch between five and two million years ago. He named the beast *Bison alticornis*. However, more finds soon changed his mind, especially a more complete skull found in Wyoming in 1888. By 1889, Marsh revised his opinions and the Pliocene buffalo became a horn-faced dinosaur.

Time of the Duckbills

One of the last and most spectacular groups of nonavian dinosaurs was the hadrosaurs. They are named after one of the earliest specimens to be studied and named, *Hadrosaurus*. "Bulky lizard" has the honor of being the first dinosaur skeleton to be excavated, described, and named in North America; Joseph Leidy did so in 1858, as described in chapter 12.

The Late Cretaceous saw a rapid diversification, or evolutionary radiation, of the hadrosaurs. They probably arose during the Late Jurassic and Early Cretaceous from the ornithopods ("bird feet") such as *Iguanodon*. Hadrosaurs are known from North and South America, Europe, Asia, and Antarctica. They seem to fall into two subgroups. The hadrosaurines were large and sturdy, while the lambeosaurines tended to be smaller. Lambeosaurines possessed elaborate crests, tubes, or plates of bone on the top of the skull, which the hadrosaurines lacked. Possible functions of these head crests are discussed later, as is evidence for hadrosaur nesting and parental care (chapter 11).

Edmonton Lizard

Hadrosaurs are known informally as "duckbills" because of the shape of the front of the mouth, which is toothless, wide, and flat, especially in forms such as *Anatotitan*. One of the largest hadrosaurines was *Edmontosaurus*, "Edmonton lizard" (see panel). It may have exceeded 30 feet (9 m) in length and weighed 4 tons. The name derives from the discovery site known regionally as

The distinctive, hollow crest of *Parasaurolophus*, a large hadrosaur of the Late Cretaceous Period, may have been capable of producing a range of loud sounds.

Lower Edmonton in southern Alberta, Canada.

Fossil skin imprints have been attributed to *Edmontosaurus*. They were formed as the skin pressed into mud that then dried; they contribute valuable information on the leathery texture and scaly appearance of *Edmontosaurus*'s dermis. Being hadrosaurine, *Edmontosaurus* lacked cranial crests. But the structure of the skull's upper snout region has led to suggestions of loose skin there, forming a nasal pouch around the airways. This might have been inflated in display when competing for mates, breeding, or intimidating enemies.

The Asian hadrosaur *Shantungosaurus*, "Shandong lizard," was very similar to *Edmontosaurus* in most respects, yet even larger. It may have exceeded 45 feet (almost 14 m) in length and weighed in excess of 8 tons. It too had a cavity near its nostrils that might have accommodated an inflatable nasal sac of skin.

The lambeosaurine hadrosaurs are based on *Lambeosaurus*, which lived slightly earlier, around 75 million years ago. The crest of *Lambeosaurus* is usually described as hatchet-shaped, perhaps with a rodlike spur behind it. As with *Edmontosaurus*, fossil skin impressions show the surface patterns of scales.

An *Edmontosaurus* on display at the Smithsonian Institution's National Museum of National History.

CHAPTER 6

EXTREMELY EXTINCT

EXTINCTION IS FOREVER. Extinction is also inevitable; it is essential for evolution. As climate and other environmental factors change, plants and animals must adapt to prevailing conditions. Usually conditions alter with imperceptible slowness, but at other times change occurs with startling rapidity. These ongoing variations drive the continuing evolution of new forms, while less adaptable life forms perish. The "Age of Dinosaurs" experienced all these conditions—changes both rapid and slow in climate, variations in the availability of water and food, and the rise and fall of populations, prey animals among them.

Rarely, a cataclysmic change occurs, sometimes leading to mass extinction. Our planet has experienced several mass extinctions and numerous minor ones. About 65 million years ago, dinosaurs and many other animals and plants were caught up in one. Exactly what happened and why are basically unknown; determining why some types of organisms survived is also difficult to discern. The changes brought an end to the Mesozoic Era, the time of "middle life," often loosely described as the "Age of Dinosaurs."

Of course, not all dinosaurs became extinct 65 million years ago. In modern scientific terms, birds are dinosaurs. So, some dinosaurs survived after all and went on to evolve and diversify.

A fanciful reconstruction shows a *Tyrannosaurus rex* fleeing from an asteroid impact. A catastrophic event like this one, or perhaps multiple natural disasters, may have caused the massive extinction at the end of the "Age of Dinosaurs."

Decreasingly Diverse

Every so often in Earth's past, mass extinctions brought an end to vast numbers of organisms. Often, extinction events are accompanied by environmental and other changes, which are shown in the geologic record as abrupt shifts in rock types. Indeed, such changes in rocks and fossils are used by geologists and paleontologists to mark the various time spans of our planet's history.

One of the most extreme mass extinctions occurred at the end of the Permian Period, some 251 million years ago. It also marked the end of the Paleozoic Era, the time of "ancient life." Estimates for the disappearance of species at the end-of-Permian event are 90 percent, 95, or even higher. Such an enormous change paved the way for the appearance of new life forms during the Triassic Period, which marked the start of the Mesozoic Era—the time when dinosaurs would come to dominate the land.

End of the Cretaceous

The final demise of the last nonbird dinosaurs coincided with the close of the Cretaceous Period. Specifically, it occurred at the end of the last stage of the Late Cretaceous, called the Maastrichtian. The Maastrichtian stage began about 70.6 million years ago and ended, according to best estimates, some 65.5 million years ago. The event is usually referred to as the end-of-Cretaceous mass extinction, which began the transition from the Cretaceous to the next period, the Paleogene. The Paleogene was the first period of the era known as the Cenozoic, "recent life."

The Paleogene, plus most of its succeeding period, the Neogene, were known in older geological dating protocols as the Tertiary Period. The Cretaceous Period gets its name from the Greek-derived Latin term *kreta*,

Trilobites left an extensive fossil record due to their easily fossilized exoskeletons.

referring to the thick layers of chalk laid down during this time, and is often referred to by the letter *K*. The transition between the Cretaceous, K, and the next period, formerly the Tertiary, or T, is often referred to in shorthand as the "K/T boundary," and the event as the "K/T mass extinction." More recent shorthand has this as K/Pg or C/Pg.

How Were Dinosaurs Doing?

Some large-scale surveys of fossils indicate that dinosaurs were already on the decline as the Cretaceous was moving toward its end. Certain estimates suggest that dinosaur diversity virtually halved during the last 10 million years of the period. However, other evidence contradicts this data; some of the disagreement is rooted in the selective assessment of surveys—for example, looking at well-documented fossil records in North America, but ignoring the records from other parts of the world.

Some of the later dinosaurs from 70–65 million years ago, as described on previous pages, included *Tyrannosaurus*, armored *Ankylosaurus*, horned dinosaurs such as *Triceratops* and *Torosaurus*, and hadrosaurs, or duckbills, like *Edmontosaurus*. It has been suggested that, in these cases, the latest dinosaurs were among the largest of their groups. Their size may be linked to the way such dinosaurs coped with changes in, or controlled, their body temperature. This, in turn, could provide evidence for the way climate change drove down dinosaur diversity, as explained on the following pages.

The K/T boundary is visible as a dark gray band between two layers of rock in these formations in the badlands near Drumheller, Alberta, Canada. The thin line of rock, which records the geologic shift from the Cretaceous to what was formerly known as the Tertiary Period, can be seen in eroded sedimentary rock all over the world.

Times of Change

Theories abound on how the non-avian dinosaurs became extinct at the end of the Cretaceous Period. Did an exploding star—a supernova—in deep space blast the planet with deadly radiation? Did a plague of certain mammals eat dinosaur eggs? However fanciful these ideas, a sensible proposal must address the fact that not only did nonbird dinosaurs disappear but so did many other groups of animals and plants, while others survived.

What is known in detail about the dinosaurs' demise is limited. How long this extinction took is difficult to say—a few minutes, one year, a century, a millennium, even a million years. Did the extinction happen simultaneously on all continents or was it progressive, moving from one land mass to another? There may never be definitive answers, since in many regions, rocks and fossils from the final, critical part of the Cretaceous Period simply have not been preserved.

New Climates

The concept of climate change is only too familiar in today's world. Fossils and rocks show that climates have changed enormously in the past, from hot and arid phases worldwide, to the deep cold of ice ages. One driving force for this process is the incredibly slow but irresistible movements of land masses around the globe. The theory of plate tectonics describes how giant curved sections of Earth's surface, known as lithospheric plates, slide on the semi-molten substance beneath them. As this happens, land and sea levels alter, some oceans open while others close, and ocean currents and wind patterns—which are closely linked to sea and land cover—also modify.

Striations in the rock layers of the Grand Canyon and similar features elsewhere provide paleontologists with a geologic calendar, allowing scientists to accurately date any fossils found within.

Toward the end of the Cretaceous Period, several large inland seas were drying up, especially in Asia and North America. Great water bodies help to moderate climates as the waters flow and mix, acting as thermal sinks for storing heat and releasing it over long periods. This evens out the effects of daily, monthly, and seasonal changes in temperature. Land warms and cools much more rapidly and regionally compared with water masses. So as land increased in surface area during the Cretaceous, climates became more variable. Plant fossils show a trend from tropical types to cooler-adapted forms. Day, night, and seasonal temperature ranges increased, as seen in the continental climates today in the centers of large land masses. This trend toward harsher, more extreme climates put a strain on organisms.

Volcanic Activity

Another area of interest is the role of volcanism, or volcanic eruptions. For example, the Deccan Traps, incorporating the Western Ghats, are a vast area of more than 200,000 square miles (500,000 sq km) of volcanic rock in west-central India. They formed when lava erupted and solidified near the close of the Cretaceous, about 66 million years ago. Volcanic outpourings on such a massive scale would be accompanied by sulphurous fumes, ash, and other ejecta of huge magnitude. Such activity may have soured the air and dimmed the Sun, adding to the stresses on organisms already struggling with the cooling, more varied climate.

The eruption of Mount St. Helens in 1980 killed 50 people and caused disruption for miles, but is only a pale example of the type of volcanic activity that accompanied or helped to cause the K/T mass extinction.

Disaster Strikes

One of the most extreme proposed explanations for the end-of-Cretaceous mass extinction involves a massive rocky body from space, an asteroid, that hit Earth. In the late 1970s, physicist Luis Alvarez, his geologist son Walter, and colleagues identified a layer at the K/T boundary in core samples from the sea floor off the coast of Italy. Chemical analyses of the layer, found in various locations worldwide, showed an unusual richness in iridium. This metal is rare at Earth's crust—but relatively common in certain meteorites and other space rocks. Calculations estimate that an object capable of causing the iridium-rich boundary layer would be some 6 miles (10 km) across.

The idea grew of a massive collision followed by an "asteroid winter." The impact would throw up colossal clouds of debris, dust, and other substances, darkening the skies for months or years. With the Sun's light and heat blotted out, plants could not grow and photosynthesize. They withered in the cool gloom, thereby depriving herbivorous animals of food. Without herbivores as prey, hunger followed for carnivores, as the disturbance worked its way along food chains and webs. Lowered temperatures slowed or stopped "cold-blooded" animals.

The strength of the impact could have set off earthquakes, fractured the crust to allow volcanic eruptions, triggered giant tsunami waves that flooded the land, and showered hot debris to torch the landscape. Some type of rapid greenhouse effect and years of acid rain are further

An asteroid colliding with Earth can radically alter or even completely destroy life on the planet. The asteroid that most scientists believe caused the K/T Extinction probably looked similar to this asteroid, named Ida, which travels in the asteroid belt between the planets Mars and Jupiter.

suggestions. Overall, the projected scene was one of massive climatic and ecological disruption.

Culprit Crater

If such an awesome impact took place, then where did it strike? A site has been identified as the Chicxulub crater, at the coast of Yucatan, Mexico. The buried crater remnant is the correct age, about 65 million years old, and has been measured at around 110 miles (175 km) across, perhaps with an outer ring or secondary crater almost 200 miles (320 km) in diameter. It is now under the Yucatan land peninsula and the bed of the Caribbean Sea. The crater's size and shape, and other strands of evidence, suggest that an asteroid struck at an angle to the horizontal of 20 to 30 degrees—a low incline to the horizon. Geological evidence includes tektites (glassy "beads" formed by suddenly heated rock ejected from the impact site and then cooled) and other "shocked" metamorphic rocks known to form under tremendous physical extremes.

Evidence for an end-of-Cretaceous asteroid impact is persuasive. Coming on top of an already changing climate, it could have been the ultimate blow to dinosaurs. But of the large and diverse array of Late Cretaceous fauna and flora, why did some die yet others survive?

This NASA image of the Yucatan peninsula in Mexico shows the semi-circle depression on the coastline, thought to be the site of a massive asteroid strike—perhaps the one that caused or exacerbated the extinction at the end of the "Age of Dinosaurs."

Died, Survived

Flying *Pteranodons* and a herd of titanosaurs flee across the ruined Cretaceous landscape, but neither flight nor size saved these creatures from destruction.

The mass extinction of 65 million years ago saw far more than the end of nonbird dinosaurs. Numerous other groups of vertebrate animals were wiped out; some of these had already been in decline. Groups that disappeared included the dinosaurs' winged archosaur cousins, the pterosaurs, and many large, predatory sea reptiles such as the long-necked plesiosaurs and their shorter-necked close relations, the pliosaurs. Other casualties were the fearsome, huge-mouthed, long-fanged mosasaurs, which were carnivorous marine reptiles closely linked to today's monitor lizards.

A Curious Mix

The list of the disappeared is long—and may seem perplexing and contradictory. For example, various amphibians, such as frogs and sala-manders, passed through the K/T boundary with few losses. The cartilaginous fish group of sharks and rays was only mildly affected, and the bony fish group, dominant in seas today, even less so. The chelonians (turtles), croco-dilians, and lepidosaurs (lizards and snakes), continued. Among birds, some of the earlier types perished, including the well-known flightless, fish-hunting *Hesperornis*, yet more newly evolved birds persisted. As for mammals, the marsupials of the Northern Hemisphere fared poorly, but many other mammal groups were relatively unscathed.

Terrestrial flowering plants suffered a temporary dip, especially in North America, where many species became extinct; in southern lands, however, changes in species balance were more common than outright disappearance. For a time, known as the "fern spike," fern spores became very common—ferns are well-known colonizers of disturbed ground. In the sea, marine plankton was hit hard. So were animal groups such as certain bivalve shellfish. The ammonites—their curly shells an icon of prehistory—had been declining for some time and their final representatives vanished, though the similar nautilus survived.

Ecological Patterns

Many attempts have been made to decipher patterns in the groups that died or survived at the end-of-Cretaceous extinction. What is evident is tremendous ecological disruption. Food chains and webs, perhaps already in flux from climate change and other environmental stresses, were greatly altered.

With widespread destruction, the generalist omnivores and the detritivores, feeding on any kinds of food including carrion, might have benefited at the expense of those adapted to food

CRETACEOUS SURVIVORS?

Could any dinosaurs or similar creatures from the Cretaceous still hang on in the modern world? Intriguing tales emerge from remote areas. In the dense rainforests of West and Central Africa are legends of a sauropodlike beast known as Mokele-mbembe. The deep lake of Loch Ness, Scotland, is famed for its "monster," usually described as a long-necked, tubby-bodied, four-flippered creature similar to a plesiosaur. Perhaps sadly, none of these is supported by hard science. The chances are extremely nanoscopic that a breeding colony of large animals has survived all the environmental changes over the past 65 million years, including ice ages, and also escaped detection by all manner of modern technologies.

chains based on green plant photosynthesis. Crocodiles might have scavenged in swamps, and smaller animals could survive by eating seeds, roots, and other plant parts, or insects and worms that subsisted on similar food scraps. But big obligate herbivores would not have had enough food. For example, *Triceratops* had few plants to crop, and, as a consequence, *Tyrannosaurus* also went hungry.

Many puzzles remain about the end-of-Cretaceous mass extinction. The selectivity of who died and who survived is a continuing problem for a cohesive scientific theory. Many scientists hope that further discoveries will shed more light on that dark time.

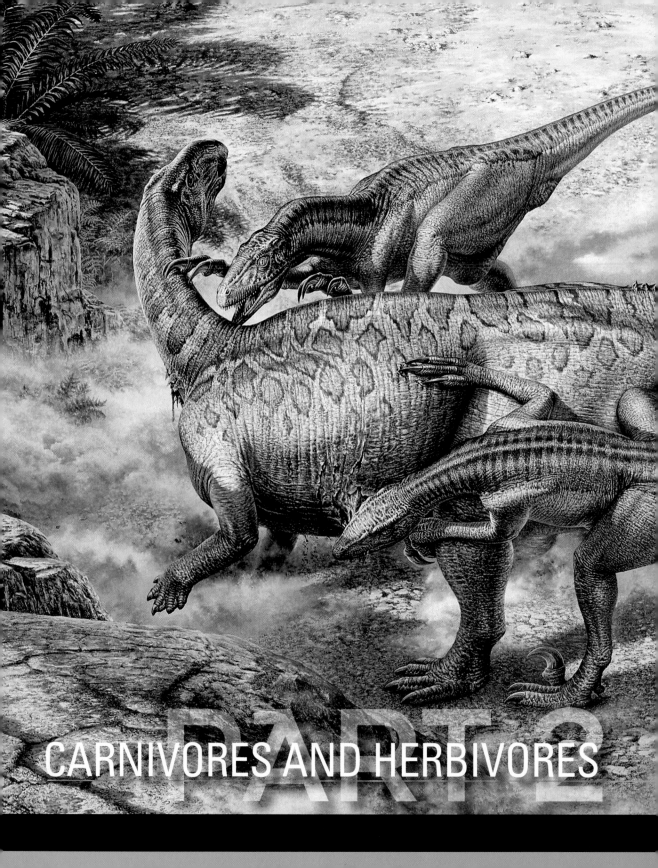

CARNIVORES AND HERBIVORES

CHAPTER 7

ON THE PROWL

FEARSOME BUT MAGNIFICENT, no dinosaurs spark our interest quite like the carnivores. Known as theropod dinosaurs, they may be large like *Tyrannosaurus* or smaller like *Velociraptor*, but they will all inspire awe— and more than a few children's nightmares—as we learn more about how they lived and imagine the rest.

What scientists do know is that theropods, including modern birds, all walked on their hind feet, striding or running with their legs underneath the body rather than angled out to the side like salamanders or alligators. Many carnivorous dinosaurs had short, strong front legs that were armed with sharp claws, the better to grasp and hold smaller prey as they fought for their lives. Other large theropods had smaller front legs, but made up for them with massive, tooth-filled jaws perfect for snapping a prey animal's neck and tearing out huge chunks of flesh from the body. In addition, a few may have hunted in packs, possibly coordinating their behavior to surround and take down much larger animals.

The following sections will describe specific carnivorous dinosaurs and what we know about how they survived so many millions of years ago.

Left: A pair of adult *Aucasaurus* bring their young to hunt newly hatched titanosaurs. Whether or not these dinosaurs lived and hunted together or if they displayed parental care is largely unknown. Pages 98–99: This depiction of a coordinated assault on *Tenontosaurus* by a group of hungry *Deinonychus* assumes that the carnivores were pack hunters, not unlike modern wolves.

Hunting Techniques

Some of the most tantalizing insights into and clues about the predatory behavior of the carnivorous dinosaurs lie in fossilized tracks.

In Dinosaur Valley State Park in Texas, for example, a trackway reveals the footprints of a single predator, possibly *Acrocanthosaurus*, that overlap and sometimes obscure the underlying tracks of a large sauropod, giving the impression that the *Acrocanthosaurus* was chasing—and thereby stepping in the footprints of—the sauropod.

A site in Queensland, Australia, shows a track from a large theropod and the tracks of more than 150 small bipedal dinosaurs. Based on the shape and size of the footprints, the small dinosaurs have been identified as coelurosaurs and ornithopods, which ranged from about 5–25.5 inches (13–65 cm) tall at the hip. The large theropod's footprints, on the other hand, measured 15.7–23.6 inches (40–60 cm) long, suggesting that the dinosaur was about 8.5 feet (2.6 m) tall at the hip. The track of the theropod is just 11 steps, but it gives sufficient information to determine that the beast changed its

walking speed in that short span from 5–5.6 miles per hour (8–9 km/h) to 3.7 mph (6 km/h). While the theropod strode through the area, however, the smaller bipeds were running at high speed all in the same direction, possibly away from the predatory theropod. The trackway also indicates that the theropod changed directions quickly, providing an intriguing glimpse into this possibly predator-prey interaction.

Likewise, a trackway near London reveals both the running and walking gait, and possible velocity, of a large dinosaur (possibly a *Megalosaurus*). The dinosaur's steps switch from a run to a walk, with the steps first pointed outward and 10 feet (3 m) apart and later pointed inward and about 4.3 feet (1.3 m) apart. According to a 2002 study by Julia Day of the University of Cambridge and others, the dinosaur walked at 4.3 miles per hour (7 km/h), but could accelerate to at least 18 miles per

Scientists speculate that a collapsing sand dune buried this *Velociraptor* (right) and *Protoceratops* (left) as they fought, preserving this rare and astonishing glimpse into dinosaur interactions millions of years ago.

hour (29 km/h) when running. The trackway is only 115 feet (35 m) long, leaving scientists to wonder how much time the large carnivore could spend at higher speeds.

Paleontologists often make inferences about hunting behaviors by examining the remains of carnivores' bodies. The typical carnivorous dinosaur, for instance, was bipedal, with the strong-clawed forelimbs mentioned earlier, and also frequently possessed daggerlike teeth. Not all predatory dinosaurs had powerful front legs or sharp teeth, however. Predators with small front limbs usually had broad, massive jaws that they used to both capture and kill prey.

In one of the most famous fossil finds, discovered in Mongolia in 1971, two dinosaurs are frozen in time during their battle. The 80-million-year-old fossils depict a *Velociraptor* and a *Protoceratops* in a battle for survival. The predatory *Velociraptor* is using one of its short front arms to grasp at the head of the *Protoceratops* while thrusting its hind feet toward the herbivore's neck. The stocky *Protoceratops*, which has a neck frill like its relative *Triceratops*, is defending itself with its beaklike mouth. The fossil suggests that the *Protoceratops* had broken the *Velociraptor*'s left arm. This particular clash became immortalized when a sediment slump apparently buried the two battling beasts alive.

Tracks of *Eubrontes* dinosaurs, uncovered accidentally during excavation for a new building, are now displayed at Dinosaur State Park in Rocky Hill, Connecticut. Trackways like these can provide valuable clues to dinosaur behavior.

WERE DINOSAURS WARM-BLOODED?

For many years, dinosaurs were assumed to have been cold-blooded animals like their reptilian ancestors. Cold-blooded, or ectothermic, animals are incapable of regulating body temperature with metabolic processes and must receive heat from an external source, such as the Sun. In the 1960s, however, some scientists suggested that most, if not all, dinosaurs might have been warm-blooded, or endothermic, capable of maintaining a relatively constant body temperature independent of their surroundings. Heated debate over endothermic vs. ectothermic continued for many years. Currently, some scientists are proposing that certain dinosaurs may have fallen somewhere between, and had a metabolism that combined the energy-saving benefits of ectothermy with the on-demand, high activity levels sometimes required of endotherms.

Small but Formidable

Although *Coelophysis* did not even stand as high as the roof of a Mini Cooper, the 3-foot (0.9 m)-tall, 6-foot (1.8 m)-long carnivore was a formidable predator. This Late Triassic biped, a forerunner of the giant dinosaurs of the Jurassic Period, had powerful rear legs that propelled a sleek and relatively lightweight body, thanks to the hollow bones in its limbs. In fact, its name means "hollow form." It also had a large head with elongated jaws filled with recurved, serrated teeth, and long, sharp claws on its fingers.

One of the offending specimens of *Coelophysis*; the bones in the stomach region were interpreted for many years as evidence of cannibalism, an accusation which has been dismissed.

Accusation and Acquittal

For some time it was believed that *Coelophysis* acted cannibalistically, perhaps when the population became stressed from lack of resources. This notion was rooted primarily in the 1947 discovery by Edwin Colbert and a scientific team from the American Museum of Natural History of a massive pile of *Coelophysis* bones near Ghost Ranch in New Mexico. The pile contained the remains of hundreds of the bipeds, which apparently died together during a flash flood or some other natural disaster. Upon closer examination, one of the skeletons contained smaller bones that Colbert identified as a young *Coelophysis*. For years, museum exhibits, books, and TV shows described the predators as cannibals.

New analyses of the bones, however, suggest that *Coelophysis* had been wrongly accused. In 2006, Sterling Nesbitt and other scientists, also from the American Museum of Natural History, reexamined the same skeletons that had led to Colbert's claim and found that some of the bones within the adults' body cavities were actually those of primitive crocodiles, or crocodylomorphs, not juvenile *Coelophysis*. They did find additional bones in the adults' guts, but the bones were too shapeless to be identified as anything other than a reptile.

Like Colbert, Nesbitt's group identified the bones of a juvenile *Coelophysis* mixed in with one of the adults, but determined that the adult had fallen on top of the juvenile when it died. As the bodies of both decayed and became compressed underground, the bones were mingled, giving a superficial but inaccurate cannibalistic appearance. In addition to the Colbert specimens, the Nesbitt team also reviewed reports suggesting cannibalism among other *Coelophysis* examples, but discounted them as inconclusive, too.

Coelophysis is not the only dinosaur that has been accused of cannibalism. Some scientists view the discovery of adult bite marks on the bones of young *Tyrannosaurus rex* and *Majungasaurus crenatissimus* as evidence that these two species occasionally dined on their young. In their paper on *Coelophysis*, however, the Nesbitt group doubts the *T. rex* evidence as well. The researchers pointed out that the bite marks in the *T. rex* could have instead come from a separate *Tyrannosaurus* species that lived in the area. The evidence for cannibalism is strong in the case of the *Majungasaurus*, however. Raymond Rogers of Macalester College and other paleontologists discovered that many bones of the dinosaurs had tooth marks that matched those of their own kind. *Majungasaurus* were carnivores that grew to nearly 30 feet (9 m) long and lived in Madagascar about 70 million years ago. Whether the dinosaurs actively preyed on their own kind or only ate their carcasses is unclear.

BATTLE OF THE BRAINS

Paleontologists sometimes are able to obtain a model of a dinosaur's brain by making a cast of the brain cavity within the fossilized skull. They use these endocranial casts, or endocasts, to estimate the weight of the brain and, after considering the size of the animal, can make inferences about the intelligence of different species. Such analyses show that predators generally have larger endocasts than similarly sized prey animals, suggesting that predators were typically smarter. The higher intelligence would be required especially if, as suspected, some of the predators engaged in coordinated pack hunting. Higher intelligence is, of course, relative; even the smartest dinosaur would not be able to compete with most modern primates, or even many modern birds.

Both Hunter and Hunted

The discovery of a large number of *Coelophysis* (which is actually made up of just one species, *C. bauri*) at the 1947 New Mexico site led to some speculation that they may have been pack hunters. This theory has since been largely discounted. The small but quick bipeds probably hunted reptiles and amphibians as well as other dinosaurs. They were not, however, immune to attacks from other carnivorous animals. Predators may have included the large reptiles known as rauisuchians or phytosaurs (*phyto* means plant, but the phytosaurs were, indeed, predatory reptiles). Rauisuchians typically grew to 13–20 feet (4–6 m) long; most phytosaurs reached 10–13 feet (3–4 m) in length, although some species topped 39 feet (12 m).

An Intelligent Pack-hunter?

Perhaps more than anyone, paleontologist John Ostrom (1928–2005) of Yale's Peabody Museum of Natural History changed the way we view dinosaurs. Until he found *Deinonychus antirrhopus*—and other dinosaurs—during his expeditions in the 1960s to Wyoming and Montana, the standard perception of dinosaurs was as solitary, plodding, unintelligent beasts. In his landmark 1969 paper on the species, Ostrom described *Deinonychus* as alert, quick, and agile animals that probably hunted and lived in packs. This led to the idea that these dinosaurs might have been relatively intelligent.

The bones Ostrom found belonged to a dinosaur twice the size of *Coelophysis*. *Deinonychus antirrhopus* stood about 4.5 feet (1.4 m) tall, was 9 feet (2.7 m) long, and weighed an estimated 150 pounds (68 kg). Perhaps the most distinctive feature was a long, severely curved claw on the second toe of each foot. The genus name reflects the characteristic and means "terrible claw." The species name *antirrhopus* means "counterbalancing"—a tribute to the long, rigid tail that set off the weight of the head and upper body and possibly helped balance the dinosaur when it was attacking prey.

Hunting Methods

During his expeditions, Ostrom found four *Deinonychus* skeletons surrounding the bones of a lone *Tenontosaurus*, a herbivorous dinosaur that was double the height and length of *Deinonychus* and, at 2,000–2,500 pounds (900–1,130 kg), was more than 10 times the weight. He hypothesized that a six- or eight-member pack of *Deinonychus* hunted together to take down the larger beast, although four of them died in the process. While Ostrom's scenario has had many supporters, it has not convinced all scientists.

With teeth that were fewer and smaller than those of *Tyrannosaurus* (but were no less sharp), *Deinonychus* would have been a fearsome predator whether it hunted in packs or not.

A study published in the 2007 *Bulletin of the Peabody Museum of Natural History*, for instance, concluded that *Deinonychus* probably acted much as most present-

Modern vultures are well known for their feeding habits, flocking to dead carrion. Their ancient dinosaur relatives may have acted similarly.

day carnivores: they hunted alone, but would occasionally bump into one another when scavenging a carcass. The study points to several joint discoveries of *Deinonychus* and *Tenontosaurus* bones, which they say show evidence of the same types of skirmishes that occur between normally solitary hunters who meet at the body of a dead animal. One clue in particular is the chewed and sometimes missing bones of juvenile *Deinonychus* that, according to the study, were likely attacked by and possibly cannibalized by adult scavengers.

Killing Methods

In addition to this study challenging Ostrom's hypotheses, other scientists have proposed new ideas about how *Deinonychus* attacked their prey. Ostrom believed that the predators used their long, curved claws for slashing and disemboweling. A study in 2006, however, used a robotic device to simulate the movement of the dinosaur's hind limb and deduced that *Deinonychus* used its claws to latch onto the hide of much larger prey in the fashion of a crampon while it bit into the flesh with its small, sharp teeth. *Deinonychus* thus attacked in much the same way that predatory big cats do today, leaping onto prey and hanging on with their claws while delivering deadly bites.

SPECIFICATIONS

Dinosaur: *Deinonychus*
Meaning: "terrible claw"
Period: Early Cretaceous
Size: 9–11.4 feet (2.7–3.5 m) long, 100–150 pounds (45–68 kg)
First discovered: 1931, Montana
Characteristics:
- Carnivorous
- Biped with long forelimbs and hands, which were tipped with three sharp claws
- Large, sickle-shaped claw on the second toe of each hind foot
- Long snout with serrated, recurved teeth
- Bone structure very similar to the most primitive known bird, *Archaeopteryx*

Fish-eating Dinosaurs

One group of carnivorous, long-snouted dinosaurs in the family Spinosauridae was a terror particularly for aquatic animals. These dinosaurs had heads that resembled those of today's gavials (also known as gharials), the long- and thin-snouted crocodilians that live in rivers in and around India. Scientists believe that like the gavial, these dinosaurs ate mostly fish.

Baryonyx, a nearly complete skeleton of which was first discovered in southern England in 1983, was a bipedal animal that reached 26–29 feet (8–9 m) in length from the tip of its snout to the end of its tail, and stood approximately 12 feet (3.6 m) tall. In appearance, it looked rather like a *Tyrannosaurus* with a severely stretched-out snout. *Baryonyx*'s

mouth was filled with nearly 100 serrated teeth: 32 in the upper jaw, with twice as many smaller ones in the lower jaw. Its name, which means "heavy claw," refers to the single, foot-long (30.5 cm) claw extending from each of its thumbs.

The evidence for its diet came from the specimen's gut contents, which included scales and bones from *Lepidotes*, a ray-finned fish. With that finding, *Baryonyx* became the first known fish-eating dinosaur. Scientists suspect it hunted by ambush: it would wait on a riverbank until a fish swam by and then quickly slap its claw-tipped forelimbs into the water to capture the prey. *Baryonyx* was not, however, strictly piscivorous. The gut contents also included the bones of an *Iguanodon*, a plant-eating dinosaur that typically grew to 33–43 feet (10–13 m) long. This led to speculation that *Baryonyx* was an opportunistic carnivore that

Above: The alarmingly long jaws, filled with 100-odd sharp teeth, probably kept *Suchomimus* in good supply of fish, which was its presumed primary diet.

Opposite: *Baryonyx* hunts for fish as brachiosaurid dinosaurs munch contentedly on vegetation in the background.

DUNG TELLS TALES

Just as biologists today can tell what a grizzly bear or wolf has eaten from its dung, paleontologists can sometimes do the same with dinosaurs' fossilized scat, called "coprolites." For instance, close examination of a 17-inch-long (44 cm) coprolite, presumably from a *Tyrannosaurus* and found in Saskatchewan, revealed at least one animal in the predator's diet. The scat contained pieces of bone from a juvenile ornithischian. Ornithischians are a group of herbivorous dinosaurs that include ceratopsids and hadrosaurids. The bone fragments provided further evidence that large predatory dinosaurs were prone to kill young prey rather than adults.

would eat whatever was most readily available.

The "Crocodile Dinosaur"

Baryonyx was not the only land-living dinosaur that got its meals from the water. In 1997, paleontologist Paul Sereno of the University of Chicago led a 15-member expedition to Africa. They nearly tripped over the thumb claw of a previously unknown dinosaur lying on the ground in Niger's Ténéré Desert. The team named the 100-million-year-old animal *Suchomimus tenerensis*, "crocodile mimic from Ténéré." It had a 4-foot-long (1.2 m) narrow skull and a claw at the end of each forelimb, similar to the closely related *Baryonyx*. *Suchomimus tenerensis* was larger, however, measuring 36 feet (11 m) long. Because of the long jaw and the many large, curved teeth at the front of its jaw, scientists believe that the dinosaur probably shared *Baryonyx*'s penchant for fish. Although the team found the skeleton in the desert, in the dinosaur's time the area was thick with forests and fed with freshwater rivers.

In addition to its long snout and forelimb claws, *Suchomimus* sported burly, 4-foot-long (1.2 m) forelimbs, and, like *Baryonyx*, a low, 2-foot (0.6 m) sail, rising over its hips.

Hunting Among Big Predators

Another upright, meat-eating, predatory dinosaur was *Allosaurus* (see chapter one). Although not especially speedy, *Allosaurus*'s prey—herbivores like the 30-foot-long (9 m) *Stegosaurus* or the enormous, 90-foot-long (27 m) *Diplodocus*—were much slower. Some scientists speculate that *Allosaurus* may have hunted in packs to bring down larger animals, and possibly employed an unusual hunting method.

Emily Rayfield of the University of Cambridge used computerized axial tomography (CT) scans to build a virtual skull and then applied a technique, called finite element modeling, to determine bite forces from the fairly long and narrow skull of *Allosaurus fragilis*, one of the species of *Allosaurus*. In particular, she based her study on "Big Al," the

exceptionally complete skeleton of an *Allosaurus* discovered in Wyoming in 1991. Rayfield's analysis revealed that the dinosaur had a much weaker bite than expected and lacked a forceful enough bite to be deadly to its prey. It did, however, have an upper jaw that could tolerate extreme forces. Rayfield hypothesized that the predator lay in ambush until a prey animal happened by. It then rushed up with its mouth wide open and, using its head as a battering ram, drove the teeth of its upper jaw into the prey. With a snap of its neck, she suggested, the curved and bladelike teeth of the *Allosaurus* would tear away a chunk of skin and muscle. If they hunted in packs, several of these predators could quickly drop even the largest of herbivores.

Hunter-scavengers?

But were *Allosaurus* and other carnivorous dinosaurs predators at all? Is it possible that most of the carnivorous dinosaurs—even the mighty *Tyrannosaurus*—were mainly scavengers that sought out carcasses far more frequently than live prey? Some see evidence for a scavenging lifestyle in eyes that were small compared to skull size and unsuited for seeing far-off prey, a good sense of smell (for sniffing out rotting meat), broad teeth rather

Below: Although known for their skills in hunting game, lions will not turn down carrion. Many scientists believe carnivorous dinosaurs were similar opportunists.

Opposite: Whether hunter, scavenger, or a bit of both, *Allosaurus* was well-equipped with claws and teeth.

than the bladelike shape expected of a carnivore, small forelimbs that would be of little use in holding prey, and fairly slow running speeds.

James Farlow of Indiana University–Purdue University Fort Wayne and Thomas Holtz, Jr. of the University of Maryland, however, have provided a different viewpoint. They described the eyes as a little bigger proportionally compared with other reptiles and, overall, large enough to see quite well. A keen sense of smell, they suggested, would also be appropriate for picking up the scent of live prey, not just dead carcasses. They agreed that the *Tyrannosaurus* was no speedster, but it was likely faster than its herbivorous prey. Tackling the contention that its teeth and small forelimbs were ill-suited to predation, Holtz and Farlow countered with examples of present-day carnivores that survive quite well with broad teeth and without using their forelimbs. In summary, they suggested that *Tyrannosaurus* and other dinosaur predators probably were scavengers given the opportunity, but were not averse to hunting. While they may not have picked solo fights with giant herbivores, the scientists believe they were likely to either ambush prey animals or chase down weak or sick members of herds.

CHAPTER 8

THE VEGETARIAN OPTION

SOME HERBIVOROUS DINOSAURS, called sauropods, were the largest dinosaurs to walk the Earth. At their largest, these behemoths measured about 100 feet (30 m) long and weighed possibly 50 tons. Sauropods made their first appearance in the fossil record in the Late Triassic, but only became numerous in the Jurassic Period. They survived until the mass dinosaur extinction 65 million years ago.

Not all sauropods were so enormous. In 2006, a team led by Martin Sander of the University of Bonn announced that the large grouping of small sauropod bones discovered at a site in the Harz Mountains in 1998 were those of adults, not of juveniles as originally thought. Rings in bones, as in trees, help determine growth rate. The bones revealed that the juvenile growth spurt was long over; the "pygmy dinosaurs" or "dwarf sauropods" were fully adult *Europasaurus*. These dinosaurs reached a comparatively diminutive 18.7 feet (6 m) long and weighed only 1 ton.

Many nonsauropod herbivores were relatively small. Herbivores had varied teeth and jaw patterns, as well as differing feeding techniques. Some examples follow.

A herd of *Brachiosaurus* dinosaurs munch their way through a grove of Jurassic conifer trees. While scientists are certain that *Brachiosaurus* dinosaurs were herbivorous, it is still unknown what kinds of plants they ate; however, their height suggests a diet of high tree leaves.

Teeth by the Hundreds, All in Rows

The several species of *Edmontosaurus* were part of the hadrosaur group, an odd-looking bunch. These ornithopods had a wide "bill" resembling that of a duck, but, unlike the waterfowl, the sides of the jaws were filled with hundreds of teeth stacked on top of one another.

This placement worked well for *Edmontosaurus*. Examinations of its coprolites (fossilized dung) reveal that its diet comprised twigs, seeds, and the needles of conifers. The dino-

continuously replaced throughout the dinosaur's life.

A Versatile Anatomy

Scientists believe that this dinosaur, which could reach up to 40 feet (12 m) long, was able to walk as either a biped or a quadruped. Its hind legs were considerably stronger and longer than the front pair. *Edmontosaurus* could rear back onto its hind legs to reach the tops of trees, but could also walk on all fours with the front end of its body pitched toward the ground. The dinosaur's neck allowed it to hold its head high enough for easy

Despite its superficial resemblance to a duck's bill, the mouth of *Edmontosaurus* was filled with teeth, unlike that of a duck. The tightly packed teeth were regrown as they were worn away.

saur would use the strong muscles in its jaws and tongue to push the vegetation back and forth and from side to side. The action placed extreme pressure on the teeth, which were

forward vision even when on all fours; it also would have permitted the beast to graze easily. In fact, the front legs were equipped with a combination of pads and hooves, suggesting that it did a good deal of four-legged walking. For many years, scientists thought *Edmontosaurus* had webbed fingers and were therefore aquatic, but the supposed webbing was later discovered to be an artifact of fossilization. The notion of webbed feet was finally put to rest for good when preserved tracks of the dinosaur revealed the mittenlike print of the pad-and-hoof arrangement.

Discoveries of multiple 70-million-year-old *Edmontosaurus* skeletons have led paleontologists to believe that these dinosaurs lived in large herds, possibly migrating to better feeding locations with the seasons. Paleontologist Lawrence Lambe named the dinosaur in 1917 after its discovery in the Horseshoe Canyon formation in what was once known as Lower Edmonton in Alberta, Canada. In 2007, paleontologist Phil Currie and his team announced that they had also found another type of dinosaur—a duckbilled herbivore called *Saurolophus*—in the same Horseshoe Canyon bone bed as an *Edmontosaurus*. *Saurolophus* is distinguished from *Edmontosaurus* in part by a crest that juts from its forehead. Until the discovery of the two dinosaurs together, it was believed that

DIRECT DIET EVIDENCE

Paleontologists have used fossilized dung, or coprolites, to help determine the diets of both carnivorous and herbivorous dinosaurs. In 2005, paleobotanist Vandana Prasad and others described titanosaur sauropod coprolites that contained remnants of conifers, palms, and grasses as well as other flowering plants. Sauropods, some of Earth's heaviest land animals, apparently were not especially picky eaters, a trait that doubtless helped them eat enough to maintain their enormous size and weight.

they did not cohabitate. The 2007 finding suggested otherwise.

Tyrannosaurus Prey

Another discovery at the Edmonton site was of an *Edmontosaurus* bone bearing evidence of a *Tyrannosaurus* bite. Because the bone had healed, the discovery showed that *Tyrannosaurus* were actively hunting live *Edmontosaurus*, some of which were able to recover from the attacks. In addition, *Edmontosaurus* specimens from Wyoming were preserved in such a way that they included imprints of their skin. Analyses indicate that the dinosaurs may have had loose skin in the nose region that could possibly inflate for mating or other displays.

Chompers and Chewers

A number of long-necked, long-tailed, plant-eating dinosaurs collectively designated sauropods roamed the Earth in the Jurassic Period. They moved their massive bodies with plodding strides made with elephantlike legs. They had small heads and brains compared with their overall body size, and nostrils set back on the snout—in some species just in front of their eyes.

For many, including *Camarasaurus*—which reached 60–65 feet (18–20 m) long and 15 feet (4.6 m) tall at the hips—a long neck would have allowed the dinosaur to reach vegetation in trees or on the ground. Based on the strong, spoon-shaped, chiseled teeth that ring both of its jaws and the interlocking wear surfaces on the teeth, scientists believe the 20-ton

This *Camarasaurus* looks like it could have used a dentist—but its large, strong, jagged teeth served the dinosaur well, chomping down on tough vegetation.

Camarasaurus chomped off plants and did some chewing of tough vegetation like pine needles and possibly ferns (although these are so low in calories that some scientists dispute this claim).

Camarasaurus fossils are plentiful and have provided information on both juveniles and adults. In fact, initial discoveries of mainly juvenile specimens led to the assumption that these dinosaurs were much smaller than they are now known to be.

Differing Dentition

One of the larger sauropods that lived in the same area and at the same time as *Camarasaurus* is *Diplodocus*. This dinosaur grew to about 90 feet (27 m)—of which about a half was a whiplike tail and nearly a quarter was neck. The name *Diplodocus* means "double beam," referring to the shape of a series of bones, the chevron bones, on the underside of its tail. While *Camarasaurus* had comparatively large teeth that ran from front to back on both jaws, *Diplodocus* skulls show smaller and peg-shaped teeth only in the front of the mouth. Based on this dentition, scientists have concluded that *Diplodocus* dined on more tender vegetation, like aquatic plants, or used its smaller teeth to strip off leaves rather than to chomp off mouthfuls of vegetation as *Camarasaurus* probably did.

A close examination of the teeth of both *Diplodocus* and *Camarasaurus* provides even more detail. The teeth of *Camarasaurus* have a rough surface marked by numerous pits, while those of *Diplodocus* have only fine scratches. Some scientists attribute the difference solely to the different diet of the two dinosaurs; others believe the more pitted teeth of the *Camarasaurus* are evidence of the amount of wind-borne grit it took in. They speculate that *Camarasaurus* did most of its feeding closer to the ground, where more grit would have been on its food. Accordingly, they suspect that *Diplodocus* fed higher off the ground, avoiding much of the grit and only experiencing light scratching on its teeth.

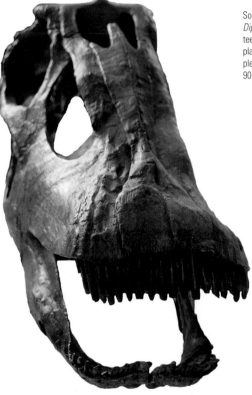

Some scientists believe that *Diplodocus* used its peglike teeth on low-growing, tender plants. It would have needed plenty of them to fuel this 90-foot-long (27 m) dinosaur.

ROLLING STONES

Some paleontologists believe that some herbivorous dinosaurs swallowed stones to help them grind up and digest the especially tough plants they ate; they point to the piles of smooth stones occasionally found in the stomach regions of dinosaur skeletons. Others disagree. Researchers Oliver Wings and P. Martin Sander of Bonn University in Germany compared the stomach stones, or gastroliths, of present-day ostriches with those discovered among the giant sauropods and concluded that the stones mingled with the dinosaur fossils were unlikely to have been used as an aid to digestion. For one, there just aren't enough stones with the sauropod bones, they say. Ostrich gastroliths have a mass of about 1 percent of the bird's weight, but the proportional weight of the stones found with giant sauropods is much lower. In addition, ostrich gastroliths never develop the polished sheen of the stones found with the sauropods. Wings and Sander did, however, find evidence of similar proportions and textures among gastroliths discovered with skeletons of oviraptorosaurs and ornithomimosaurs, suggesting that these dinosaurs did indeed ingest stones to help break down their vegetarian meals.

Making a Living on Plants

Although *Stegosaurus* may look fearsome, with its double row of tall, triangular plates rising from its neck, back, and tail—as well as the four spikes at the end of its tail—it was a plant eater, not a predator. This dinosaur, whose name means "roofed lizard" (in reference to its plates), reached about 25 feet (7 m) long and 5–5.5 tons as a full-sized adult. It had a robust body and tail, and four trunklike legs, but its head was quite small and its brain was tinier than a golf ball. *Stegosaurus* did, in fact, have only one brain—although a long-held belief suggested that the brain in the head was simply too small to control such a large beast and an expanded region of the spinal column in the hip region was a second, larger brain that controlled the dinosaur's hind limbs. The second

"brain" is no longer considered a brain at all, but scientists still disagree about its function. Some have suggested it is a network of nerves—a sacral nerve plexus—while others proposed that it may have been a storage area for fats and fatlike compounds. Most, however, consider it to be a typical enlargement of the spinal cord in the hip region.

A Plodding Browser

Stegosaurus survived by making its living off vegetation. Most scientists believe these dinosaurs browsed mosses, ferns, and other low-lying plants while walking slowly along. A controversial theory, however, proposes that the animals had the ability to raise their shorter front legs and, just as the *Edmontosaurus* did, to stand on their taller, muscular hind legs to reach higher vegetation. In this bipedal posture, *Stegosaurus* could reach plant material up to 15 feet (5 m) off the ground. The dinosaur had a long snout with a toothless beak at the front. Further back in the jaws sat a row of cheek teeth with ridges on the surface and sharp edges that formed because the teeth wore unevenly. The dinosaur probably used the beak to tear away vegetation and employed its cheek teeth to give it a coarse chop before swallowing.

Teeth as Evidence

Dinosaur teeth are often distinctive enough to be important in identifying fossils. For example, in 2007, scientists from Portugal and Spain announced the discovery of an incomplete skeleton that was identified, in part, by a single small tooth that had the prominent ridges and a pattern of wear on its tongue-side, or lingual, surface, characteristic of *Stegosaurus.* The remains included a few other bones: some vertebrae and ribs, a

piece of a hip, and a few plate fragments. The discovery proved especially valuable because the skeleton was found in Portugal, not the United States. In their paper on the finding, Fernando Escaso of the Autonomous University of Madrid and the research team called it "the first incontrovertible evidence that a member of the genus *Stegosaurus* lived outside North America." The researchers believe it is strong evidence that a land corridor at one time linked North America to southwestern Europe.

The four spikes at the end of *Stegosaurus*'s tail were almost certainly used in self-defense. The vertical arrangement shown here is likely incorrect; more probably, the spikes were positioned more horizontally.

Horned Dinosaurs

Two well-known horned dino-saurs, *Centrosaurus* and *Triceratops*, shared more in common than the crest (frill) at the back of the head and the horns above the eyes and over the snout: they were both plant-eaters.

Sharp-pointed Lizard

Centrosaurus, which reached 17–20 feet (5–6 m) long and 2.5–3 tons, was the smaller of the two. Its name, meaning "sharp-pointed lizard," makes note of the up-to-18-inch-long (47 cm) nasal horn that protruded from its snout. The other two brow horns were much smaller and located above the eyes.

Huge bone beds in Dinosaur Provincial Park in Alberta, Canada, have pro-vided many fossils of *Centrosaurus*, including a mass grave of hundreds and perhaps thou-sands of the beasts. Paleontologists believe the dinosaurs traveled in herds, one of which may have drowned as it crossed a flood-ing river. Since teeth marks as well as

The distinctive horn on *Centrosaurus* skulls may have been used for defense. The beak at the front of the mouth is a sure indication of an herbivorous diet.

actual teeth from carnivorous dino-saurs, probably *Albertosaurus*, have also been found on and among the bones, it is likely that the carnivores later came across the already-dead *Centrosaurus* herd and scavenged the bodies. *Albertosaurus* was a large-headed, long-tailed, bipedal dinosaur that shared many features with its close relative *Tyrannosaurus*. Adult *Albertosaurus* were smaller than *Tyrannosaurus*, but still reached roughly 30–33 feet (9–10 m) long.

Other Bony Arrangements

Triceratops, on the other hand, grew to 25–30 feet (8–9 m) and 5–6 tons.

Unlike *Centrosaurus*, *Triceratops*'s nasal horn was dwarfed by the long, straight, brow pair of horns that reached as much as 3 feet (0.9 m) long. *Triceratops* also had a frill that stretched up to 4 feet (1.2 m) wide and was edged in bony projections. The crest made the dinosaur look even larger.

At one time, scientists believed *Triceratops* included more than a dozen species because of differences in the fossils. Now, they attribute the differences to individual variation within only one or possibly two species. Scientists are still, however, finding new members of the family Ceratopsidae, to which both *Triceratops* and *Centrosaurus* belong. In 2001, paleontologists found an unusual skull in Alberta. After studying it for several years, in 2007 they proclaimed that it was a new species and genus: *Albertaceratops nesmoi.* This dinosaur looked almost like a cross between *Triceratops* and *Centrosaurus,* featuring the large brow horns of the *Triceratops* as well as the more ornate crest of the *Centrosaurus.*

Sharp Mouth for Plants

Both *Centrosaurus* and *Triceratops*, along with other members of the family Ceratopsidae, had a toothless beak at the front of strong jaws and also had cheek teeth set farther back. The cheek teeth were shaped like blades and were, therefore, unsuited to grinding plant material. The teeth apparently slid past each other like the blades of a scissors, shearing vegetation into pieces. The

dinosaurs also had double-rooted, self-sharpening teeth that were set in so-called dental batteries. In this arrangement, the teeth locked onto adjacent teeth to the side and also to the replacement teeth growing beneath them. Because their teeth grew continuously throughout life, these dinosaurs always had sharp tools at the ready for their next meal.

The solid frill of *Triceratops* led to the conclusion that the dinosaurs used them as shields, but comparisons with other ceratopsians have led some to suggest alternative functions, such as dominance displays.

CHAPTER 9

SELF-DEFENSE

PREDATORY DINOSAURS had a variety of combinations of large teeth for tearing, sharp claws for grasping or ripping, and strong leg muscles for running—all excellent tools for hunting their prey, which often included herbivorous dinosaurs. The average herbivore, on the other hand, was a plodding beast that lacked claws, had teeth suited for grazing on vegetation rather than for attacking, and had a comparatively minuscule brain that, it is assumed, made it less intelligent than its predators. Nevertheless, the advantage was not always with the carnivorous dinosaur.

Herbivores used a number of defensive techniques. As is common with today's herbivorous mammals, many of the plant-eating dinosaurs traveled in herds. While such groupings make the prey animals more conspicuous in general, it affords protection in many ways, including providing more eyes to scan for danger and decreasing any one individual's chance of being singled out for attack, particularly if it is at the center of the herd.

The dinosaurs described on the following pages all had defensive strategies. Some were heavily armored, some had tail clubs or spikes to repel predators, others had sharp horns to ward off their enemies. Although speed was not the norm, a few herbivorous dinosaurs had the option of running away to avoid becoming a meal.

Ankylosaurs like *Polacanthus foxii* relied on their heavy body armor, rather than speed or large herds, to protect them from predators. *Polacanthus* is a poorly known genus, but it lived in what is now southern England during the Early Cretaceous Period.

Heavy Armor

Ankylosaurs, a group of herbivorous dinosaurs, were armored with plates, spikes, and studs that helped to protect them from predators. The armor was probably a needed defense since ankylosaurs were not especially large—ranging from about 7–10 feet (2.1–3 m) in *Minmi* to at least twice that size in *Edmontonia* and others—and probably spent much of their waking hours with their heads down feeding on ferns, horsetails, small club mosses, or other low-lying vegetation. The location and analysis of ankylosaur trackways by Swiss paleontologist Christian Meyer of the University of Basel suggests that these dinosaurs could trot at 8 mph (11 kph). Although that speed is quite a feat for a dinosaur carrying a coat of weighty armor, it would not have been fast enough to outrun a typical predator.

A North American dinosaur of the Late Cretaceous Period, *Edmontonia* may have used its impressive body armor to fend off predatory dinosaurs like *Tyrannosaurus rex* and *Albertosaurus*.

Edmontonia and *Sauropelta*

Edmontonia was one of the most heavily armored of the ankylosaurs. It was named for the location where its fossil skeleton was found: the Edmonton Formation (now called the Horseshoe Canyon Formation) in Alberta, Canada. Adults could reach 23–25 feet (7–7.6 m) long and weigh roughly 3.5–4 tons (3,200–3,600 kg). Like other ankylosaurs, it walked on all four feet with its short legs carrying its body quite low to the ground. While its back and tail were covered with small, thick, and solid bony plates, the most notable features on this member of the family Nodosauridae were on the neck and shoulders: large bony plates (osteoderms) along with spikes, some of which pointed forward. This armor arrangement has caused paleontologists to speculate that the animal turned to face its predators head on in order to take full advantage of the armor at the front end of its body and its forward-facing spikes.

Another ankylosaur in the family Nodosauridae was *Sauropelta*, which grew to about 16.5 feet in length (5 m) and weighed 1–1.5 tons (900–1,400 kg). Like *Edmontonia*, its largest spikes were at its shoulders. In addition, it had cone-shaped spikes on its neck and a line of smaller spikes along each side of its leathery-skinned body that stretched onto its tail. Also like *Edmontonia*, its best defense would have been to turn its spiked front end toward an attacker.

Gastonia and Its Relatives

Gastonia, an unusual-looking ankylosaur that was once relegated to its own family (Polacanthidae) was named by paleontologist James Kirkland for dinosaur enthusiast Robert Gaston. The 13-to-16.4-foot-long (4–5 m) beast had armor that included a double row of spikes running halfway down the center of its back and a few shorter spikes on the neck and head. In addition to this forward protection, it also had fused plates of armor that formed a shield over its hips and provided a bit of security to the back of its body.

The assignment of *Gastonia* and the similar species *Mymoorapelta* and *Polacanthus* to their own family was proposed because the three dinosaurs did not quite fit into the

---

MALE VS. FEMALE

Fossils seldom provide clues about gender or whether males and females of a dinosaur species had any gender-specific characteristics. Sometimes, however, enough fossils are found to show two distinct variations, perhaps large vs. small frills or spikes, or differently oriented horns. A few examples of possible male-female differences are: *Edmontonia*, one with larger shoulder spikes; *Heterodontosaurus*, one with larger canine teeth; and *Protoceratops*, one lacking a small nasal bump. In the first two instances, the trait is assumed to be that of a male. The latter is suspected to be a female characteristic. Distinguishing between the fossils can be very tricky, however. A study in 2006, for instance, showed that what were thought to be male and female *Corythosaurus* were actually not separate genders but separate species: one in the genus *Corythosaurus* and the other in *Lambeosaurus*.

---

other two existing ankylosaur families, Nodosauridae and Ankylosauridae. For example, they had four small horns on a triangular head and a tail without a club on its end. The head horns and triangular head are typical of ankylosaurids, but the lack of a tail club is a feature of nodosaurids, which had pear-shaped heads sporting narrower snouts than ankylosaurids. Now, however, *Gastonia*, *Mymoorapelta*, and *Polacanthus* are often grouped within the family Ankylosauridae.

Tails for Defense

Many dinosaurs in the family Ankylosauridae sported a heavy, bony club on the end of the tail.

Euoplocephalus

One of the larger and the best known of the ankylosaurids is *Euoplocephalus* (sometimes called *Scolosaurus*), a stout, armored dinosaur that reached up to 23 feet (7 m) in length. Its name means "well- or truly armored head." The rather extensive fossil record for this animal clearly reveals its protective coat of armor that covered the back and sides of its low-slung

The massive bony structure at the end of *Euoplocephalus*'s tail would have provided this Late Cretaceous, North American ankylosaur with a formidable defense against predators.

body and even extended to its eyelids. Despite all of the armor, *Euoplocephalus* was quite agile because the armor plates were separated by flexible skin that allowed fairly free movement. Trackways of ankylosaurids suggest that while *Euoplocephalus* may not have been a fast sprinter, it could probably move along at a decent clip.

One of its most notable features is the large mass of bone at the end of its tail. In fact, the tail club is almost as big as its head. Fossils indicate that the tail was a muscular structure that the *Euoplocephalus* held in a raised position, but could also swing powerfully if required. Any predator that risked an attack on the dinosaur would have received a fierce blow from its clubbed tail, which was very stiff because of its skeletal design. The vertebrae just preceding the tail were fused into a strong rodlike structure, and the two enlarged bony nodules in the club were fused to the tail vertebrae. As a result, a swing of the tail would be more like a wallop from a bat than a zing from a whip.

Ankylosaurus

An even larger ankylosaurid was *Ankylosaurus*, a name that means "fused lizard." This dinosaur grew to 36 feet (11 m) in length and 4 tons—about two-thirds the weight of *Tyrannosaurus* (fossils of which have been found in the same general area as *Ankylosaurus*). Like *Euoplocephalus*, *Ankylosaurus* had a large tail club and a body with armored plates somewhat akin to those on the bodies of today's crocodiles. *Ankylosaurus* also shared with

Euoplocephalus the set of four horns on its head, but those of *Ankylosaurus* were more prominent. The 36-foot-long dinosaur also had a stiff tail that it was able to swing it back and forth, no doubt to deliver a mighty blow to any predator that came a bit too close.

Other Tail Tales

Over the years, some paleontologists have speculated that the ankylosaurids were not the only dinosaurs with defensive tails. Some suggested that the tip of the long and tapering tail on *Apatosaurus* and other sauropods in the family Diplodocidae would have been excellent weapons for whipping at attackers—or possibly for startling an approaching menace by flicking the tail through the air, thus creating a loud cracking sound similar to that produced by the snapping of a

POWERFUL TAIL

In 2002, scientists learned more about the defensive capabilities of *Stegosaurus* when a research team led by Frank Sanders of the Denver Museum of Natural History reported at a meeting of the Society of Vertebrate Paleontology that the dinosaur could have used its spike-tipped tail to lash out at predators. The researchers analyzed fossils of the species *Stegosaurus stenops*, concentrating on the four, 3-foot-long (1 m) spikes at the end of its tail, as well as the structure of the tail. They maintained that the animal could swing its tail back and forth and deliver a whack mighty enough to poke the spikes through a predator's skin and into the bone.

bullwhip. The argument for such tail whipping came under scrutiny when later research indicated that such an action would likely have been quite painful to the sauropods.

This reconstruction of an *Ankylosaurus* demonstrates how the dinosaur's body armor protected it virtually on all sides.

Horns and Frills

Members of two families, Protoceratopsidae and Ceratopsidae, are known for the generally large frills that extend up and out from the back of the head and for the brow and nasal horns seen in several species. The dinosaurs ranged from about 4–5 feet long (1–2 m) in *Bagaceratops* to 25–30 feet (7.6–9.1 m) in *Triceratops*.

Battle Horns

Depending on the species, the brow and nasal horns may have been straight, curled, prominent, small, or missing altogether. *Leptoceratops*, for instance, had no horns and only a small frill. In *Protoceratops*, which grew to about 10 feet (3 m) long, only some—thought to be the males—had a small nasal bump, and neither sex had brow horns. At the other end of the scale, *Torosaurus* and *Triceratops* each

had long, pointed brow horns that could reach up to 3 feet long (1 m) in *Triceratops*. These spiky brow horns were likely formidable defensive weapons against predators, but they also may have been used in intraspecies (within-species) rivalries, likely between males that may have pushed at each other when fighting over breeding rights. Discoveries of ceratopsid frills with scarred-over puncture wounds suggest that some did, indeed, engage in what were, at least, shoving matches if not more violent struggles.

One of the most unusual looking ceratopsids was *Einiosaurus*, a name that means "bison lizard." A 20-foot-long (6.1 m) dinosaur with the typical stout body of other members of the family, it had short and nubby brow horns, but a large nasal horn. In juveniles, the horn stood upright, but as the creature aged, the horn turned distinctly downward, curving to a 90-degree angle in fully grown adults.

Two *Protoceratops*, on display in the American Museum of Natural History, alongside a clutch of eggs. *Protoceratops* may not have used its frill for defense, but it could certainly use its beak to fight off predators. These *Protoceratops* were once thought to be defending these eggs from *Oviraptor*, but it has since been determined that the eggs belonged, in fact, to *Oviraptor*.

SPECIFICATIONS

Dinosaur: _Triceratops_
Meaning: "three-horned face"
Order: Ornithischia
Family: Ceratopsidae
Period: Late Cretaceous
Size: 25–30 feet (8–9 m) long and 5–6 tons
First discovered: 1887, near Denver, Colorado
Region: Western United States and Canada,
    including Colorado, Montana, Wyoming,
    Alberta, and Saskatchewan
Characteristics:
- Herbivorous, likely eating tough,
  fibrous plants
- Stocky quadruped with a short tail
- Narrow head with a beak at the end
  of the jaws
- Bladelike teeth
- Two large, straight brow horns reaching
  up to 3 feet (0.9 m) long
- One shorter nasal horn in the middle
  of the snout
- Rounded, solid (unperforated) frill edged
  with small, bony studs and stretching up
  to 7 feet (2.5 m) wide

Frills for Show?

While the erect and sharp horns on many ceratopsids appear to have had at least some defensive function, the purpose of the frills is less obvious. Some, but not all, species had frills adorned with long, pointed horns. _Styracosaurus_, a name that means "spiked lizard," had a half dozen very noticeable horns lining the top edge of its frill. Likewise, _Einiosaurus_ sported a pair of large frill horns. Other ceratopsids, however, had large frills that lacked horns. One was _Torosaurus_, which had an enormous, rounded frill that was longer than its entire head, but did not have so much as a bony stud on its perimeter. This discrepancy in shapes and sizes has led many paleontologists to suspect that the frill was not used as a defensive weapon—although the horned frills may have deterred some predators—but rather as a display item, possibly to make the dinosaur look larger to rival males, or to potential nest-raiding predators, or simply to identify to others of the same species that the dinosaur was one of their number. Although mainly conjecture, some scientists believe that, at least in some species, males may have had larger frills than females, a hypothesis that would support the idea that the frills had a more important role for males, possibly for male-to-male displays. Scientists suspect that both the protoceratopsids and ceratopsids likely took full advantage of their frills, regardless of the frill size or the presence of horns upon it, by tilting the head down to fully show off its size.

Triceratops shows off its massive frill and impressive horns; even herbivorous dinosaurs could be fearsome.

Butting Heads

The bipedal, thick-headed *Stegoceras* were the bighorn sheep of their day. They raced toward one another, and with a mighty crack, butted heads in battles for social or sexual dominance. Or did they?

Stegoceras and *Pachycephalosaurus*

Stegoceras (not to be confused with *Stegosaurus*) were 7-foot-long (2 m) dinosaurs with powerful hind limbs and much smaller forelimbs. Their name means "roof horn" and refers to the very thick dome of bone at the top of its skull. In some fossils, the dome is much lower and flatter than in others, suggesting that males and females may have been distinguishable. Another species in the family Pachycephalosauridae was the eponymous *Pachycephalosaurus*, a simi-

This *Stygimoloch*, with its thick skull and bony head spikes, may have been a male. Although judging sexual dimorphism, or appearance differences due to gender, is difficult with extinct animals, males may have had more impressive head structures for display and mating purposes.

larly shaped but much larger dinosaur at 26 feet (8 m) long. As implied by its name, which means "thick-headed lizard," it, too, had a heavily domed head. While the dome of *Stegoceras* did not fully encompass the rear of the skull, the dome of *Pachycephalosaurus* did. Both skulls, nonetheless, led to the same conclusion: these dinosaurs used their heads as battering rams.

Not So Fast

The notion of head-butting dinosaurs held for many years, but received a serious challenge in 1998 when Mark Goodwin of the Museum of Paleontology at the University of California–Berkeley and others determined that a head-to-head collision between two adult dinosaurs would have caused at least a concussion, if not more serious injury, and perhaps death. Goodwin included a more recently discovered pachycephalosaurid, *Stygimoloch*, in his study. *Stygimoloch* was a 7-foot-long (2 m) dinosaur with a bony skull dome that had tall spikes at the back edge. Goodwin found significant and suggestive discrepancies between the skulls of the dinosaurs and those of the head-butting sheep living today. Bighorn sheep have strong necks, supporting broad heads equipped with shock-absorbing chambers; but

Pachycephalosaurids, on the other hand, had skulls that were tall and narrow and lacked such protective structures.

Since that 1998 research, some have suggested that spongy tissue found in the domes of some fossilized pachycephalosaurid skulls could have provided sufficient shock absorption. Goodwin and John Horner of the Museum of the Rockies at the University of Montana conducted a follow-up study of growth and development of pachycephalosaurids; in 2004, they reported that the tissue is seen only in juveniles and gradually declines until it disappears completely in the skulls of adults, the age group that would have engaged in the head-butting behavior.

Side Butting?

Their findings, however, do not rule out some form of butting. Some scientists have suggested that Stegoceras and other pachycephalosaurids may have used their thickly skulled heads to push against each other rather than to run into each other at full speed. Another hypothesis is that the dinosaurs rammed not into the hard head but into the side of a fellow pachycephalosaurid in contests for social status or mating rights. Both of these ideas will likely remain just that, since the fossil record is unlikely to ever show any evidence supporting or refuting such long-ago skirmishes.

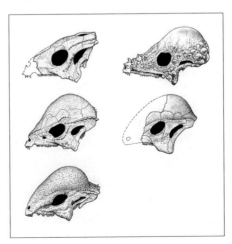

The enlarged bony domes on the skulls of these dinosaurs help to identify them as pachycephalosaurs, or "boneheads." Why their heads developed in such a fashion remains unknown.

Run, *Gallimimus*, Run!

The difficulties in estimating a dinosaur's speed are numerous. Because dinosaurs are extinct, scientists must rely on indirect information, which may include fossils of leg and other bones that could give clues to body size and overall mass, as well as how the dinosaur walked and the power of its musculature. Some scientists have also derived speed estimates by comparing dinosaurs with present-day animals of similar size, weight, and musculature. Of course, such comparisons have their limits and are subject to different interpretations.

An *Ornithomimus* ("ostrich mimic") flees across a barren plain. Likely very fast and agile, these dinosaurs probably depended on speed to evade predators.

Trackway Evidence

Trace fossils, especially trackways that show the actual stride length of a dinosaur, have become especially useful in estimating a dinosaur's speed. Even this type of rare but highly valuable evidence can be ambiguous. Often, identifying the exact species from the tracks is impossible, and scientists can only make general identifications, such as "a small bipedal dinosaur" or "a large theropod." In addition, the tracks frequently were originally made in mud. While mud permits a deep imprint, it is an imprecise medium for preserving the exact dimensions and details of the dinosaur's foot. Also, the dinosaur may have had to step differently when moving in the mud vs. on dry land; thus the animal's maximum speed might not be reflected in the fossil evidence.

Despite these variables, scientists are able to determine the relative running speeds of dinosaurs—and which dinosaurs were among the fastest—even if they cannot precisely state their running speed.

Speedy Attributes

Gallimimus is one of the species that counters the image of dinosaurs as huge, heavy brutes plodding along the ground in earth-shaking steps. This is the dinosaur shown in the movie *Jurassic Park* racing in a herd through a field just before a *Tyrannosaurus rex* makes its appearance. As shown in the movie, *Gallimimus* was not enormous but it was fast. In size, *Gallimimus* measured about 17–20 feet (6–7 m) long and weighed up to 1,000 pounds (454 kg). Its speed is assumed to have been its greatest defense against predators. With long, strong legs and hollow bones that made the body light, *Gallimimus* has been estimated to run at speeds of 25 to 50 mph (40–80 km/h). Even at the lower end of the scale, as is generally proposed, that speed would have made it one of the fastest dinosaurs.

Another member of *Gallimimus*'s family, Ornithomimidae, was *Struthiomimus*. A bit smaller, but otherwise similar in overall body shape, *Struthiomimus* was quite fast, too, and likely used its speed to evade predators.

Hypsilophodon

Gallimimus and *Struthiomimus* were both theropods in the order Saurischia, but theropods were not the only swift dinosaurs. An example is the 6-to-8-foot-long (1.8–2.4 m) herbivore *Hypsilophodon* in the order Ornithischia. A bipedal dinosaur, it ran on powerful hind legs with its body hunched forward so that it stood only about 3 feet tall. In the late nineteenth century, some paleontologists proposed the idea that *Hypsilophodon* was able to climb trees. The notion remained for many years, but an extensive examination of the dinosaur in 1974 by paleontologist Peter Galton of the University of Bridgeport showed that it was not arboreal and that it remained on the ground. Like many herbivorous dinosaurs as well as herbivorous mammals on Earth today, *Hypsilophodon* may have lived in groups.

Hypsilophodon fossils are found mostly in Europe and date to the Early Cretaceous Period. Its name, which means "high ridge tooth," derives from its long cheek teeth.

EXTREME LIFESTYLES

PART 3

CHAPTER 10

SURVIVAL TACTICS

ANY CHILD WITH A SET OF TOY DINOSAURS no doubt groups several species together, perhaps creating herds of favorites like *Stegosaurus*, *Triceratops*, and *Apatosaurus*. In reality, paleontologists have a far from complete picture of the alliances and movements of dinosaurs. Some of their best information comes from trackways—preserved impressions of dinosaur footfalls—that seem to indicate mixed-species herds and possibly long-distance movements, including annual migrations.

Studies of herds, migrations, and how nonmigrating polar dinosaurs may have survived the long cold winters have yielded a number of clues, but much work is left to be done. In particular, scientists continue investigating the North Slope of Alaska and southeastern Australia, both of which were polar regions during the dinosaurs' era. Both areas contain fossil evidence of various species. In addition, paleontologists are making new discoveries in Siberia, the Yukon, parts of the Canadian Arctic, New Zealand, and other areas to learn how dinosaurs coped with extreme conditions and survived for so many millions of years.

Left: A herd of *Iguanodon*, flanked by *Hypsilophodons*, makes its way down a Cretaceous floodplain. Fossilized tracks of certain dinosaurs suggest that they traveled in herds and may have migrated, following riverbanks. Pages 134–135: *Triceratops*, *Pachyrhinosaurus*, and *Styracosaurus* (from left to right) are examples of ceratopsians, herbivorous quadrupeds from the Cretaceous Period whose frills and horns make them some of the most recognizable of dinosaur groups.

Did They Migrate?

As discoveries of fossils and trackways have mounted over the years, scientists have begun to offer hypotheses about dinosaur movements, including the animals' possible migration.

Polar Finds

In 1960, the discovery of an ornithopod trackway in Svalbard, a chain of islands located in the Arctic Ocean north of mainland Norway, provided definitive evidence that dinosaurs had once lived in polar regions. Dinosaur footprints have since been found in polar areas of Siberia and North America.

As these areas were also within the Arctic Circle in the dinosaurs' time, speculation increased about the various techniques that dinosaurs used to survive harsher northern climates. Migration was inevitably proposed as one possible survival strategy.

Edmontosaurus

Fossils of the hadrosaur *Edmontosaurus* have been found along an Alaskan river north of the Arctic Circle. Dinosaurs living in such a location would have to weather a number of hardships to survive the polar climate, including a lack of vegetation, increased darkness, and cool average temperatures. There is much that paleontologists do not yet know about life lived at such extremes during prehistoric times. *Edmontosaurus* could have stayed above the Arctic Circle year-round, and perhaps weathered the cold through physiological means. Plant life may have been plentiful enough to live on all year, and with its strong jaws and hundreds of teeth, *Edmontosaurus* could certainly break down hardy northern vegetation. That said, some paleontologists believe that the environment must have been too harsh, and that *Edmontosaurus* migrated south for the winter months

One of the largest of known hadrosaurs, *Edmontosaurus* was capable, scientists believe, of covering vast distances, traveling for long periods at a speed of about 15 miles per hour (25 km/h). Such physical capabilities would be useful if *Edmontosaurus* were a migratory dinosaur, as some scientists theorize.

to find more sufficient vegetation. The migration may have been analogous to that of modern-day caribou, which also begin to trek south as winter approaches. Bones of *Edmontosaurus* have been found as far south as Wyoming, although it is impossible to say whether these dinosaurs were part of herds that participated in migrations to and from the Arctic Circle.

DINOSAUR FREEWAY

Near Clayton Lake in northeastern New Mexico, dozens of dinosaur trackways follow what in early-to-mid-Cretaceous times was a shoreline of the Western Interior Seaway that sliced through the center of North America. In some trackways, the footprints are headed north; in others they are moving southward. The tracks belong to various species of ornithopods, suggesting that they traveled and possibly migrated in mixed-species herds.

Pachyrhinosaurus

Another dinosaur that some speculate migrated from colder to warmer climes and back is the *Pachyrhinosaurus*. Its name, which means "thick-nosed lizard," calls attention to its broad snout, which was topped not with a horn like the closely related *Triceratops* and *Torosaurus*, but with a flat, bony pad, called a boss. Two smaller bosses sat at the brow. *Pachyrhinosaurus* may have used the bosses to push against one another in intraspecies shoving contests. A *Pachyrhinosaurus* bone bed discovered in Alberta, Canada, included fossils from both juveniles and adults, implying that these dinosaurs traveled in mixed-age herds. The location of these fossils and others in Alaska has led to the theory that *Pachyrhinosaurus,* may have migrated north and south with the seasons, but no incontrovertible evidence yet supports this idea.

Humans are used to seeing dinosaurs migrate—every year in North America, for instance, flocks of Canadian geese travel from northern summer habitats to southern winter ones, and back.

Mixed Herds

Numerous studies of fossil beds and trackways provide strong evidence that certain dinosaurs lived in herds. Depending on the species, the makeup of the herd differed.

Mixed Herds

Possible evidence for herds of more than one dinosaur species came from a study published in 2002 by paleontologist Julia Day of the University of Oxford and others. The researchers evaluated more than three dozen dinosaur trackways, some of them nearly 600 feet (180 m) long, all grouped at one site in Oxfordshire, England. The trackways, estimated to have been made 163 million years ago during the Middle Jurassic, are parallel and show the dinosaurs all moving in the same direction.

The researchers believe that the trackways followed a long-ago shoreline and were made during the few hours between two consecutive high tides. This, according to the research group, suggests that they are all part of the same herd. Their contention is controversial, however, and many scientists do not agree that the researchers have conclusive proof that the tracks were made at the same time. A close review of the footprints revealed two distinct tracks, one with a narrow, pigeon-toed stance, and imprints of claws; a second with a wide, toes-pointed-out stance but no claws. According to the study, this verifies that the herd included at least two different species of sauropods, one of which, surprisingly, was a species belonging to the group of huge sauropods known as titanosaurs. Until the study, titanosaurs were thought to have first appeared on Earth some 12 million years later.

In addition to the sauropod trackways, nearby footprints of predatory

Did sauropods travel together? The *Diplodocus, Camarasaurus,* and *Brachiosaurus* visible here may not have been strangers —although any such herd must have regularly eaten through forests of trees.

theropod dinosaurs led the researchers to speculate that the mixed herd may have served a defensive role and that the herd's one-way movement may have been triggered by the theropod threat. A second hypothesis suggested that the movement might have been migratory in nature.

Adults Only

In some cases, herds appear to have had age restrictions: Juveniles seem to have stayed together and separate from adults until they grew to about half the size of the adults. This age distinction is often seen in groups of *Protoceratops*, hadrosaurs like *Maiasaura* and *Hypacrosaurus*, and the ankylosaur *Pinacosaurus*, among others. One line of reasoning holds that the adults were not shunning the juveniles so much as the juveniles were unable to keep up with the older and presumably faster-moving herd until the youngsters were of sufficient size. Other dinosaurs, such as *Apatosaurus* and other sauropods apparently had mixed-age herds.

Were They Herds?

Some paleontologists are more skeptical of trackway evidence and inferences, noting that the footprints in a trackway may not confirm simultaneous traffic, but may show footfalls made at different times. The apparent mixed herd, there-

Apatosaurus tracks in the Colorado portion of the Morrison Formation may suggest herding behavior.

ODD TRACKWAYS

A number of unusual trackways show only the front feet of dinosaurs. Although the first impression may be that the dinosaurs were doing handstands, computer and laboratory studies indicate they were caused by dinosaurs partially floating in water. Separate studies by University of Calgary paleontologist Donald Henderson and by Jeffrey Wilson and Daniel Fisher of the University of Michigan suggest that the trackways could have been made by sauropods that were wading through shallow or slowly rising water. Their analyses demonstrated that under certain conditions, the rear half of the body would be more buoyant than the front, causing the dinosaurs to put more pressure on their front legs, thus leaving the odd tracks behind.

fore, may instead be the combination of individuals or small same-species groups traveling across a particular area over many hours, even several days, but not as part of one cohesive group. Generally, indications of herding behavior in trackways include: all footprints heading in the same direction rather than crossing one another's paths; group-wide changes in direction; and similar definition in the tracks, indicating that they were made at about the same time.

Surviving in a Harsh Climate

On Alaska's North Slope during the Cretaceous Period, dinosaurs faced a number of challenges. Although temperatures may not have been as cold as they are now, they still would have dropped below freezing during the winter. As the dark, cold months approached, plant life would have become less available for any herbivores that remained in the area. While the region was home to coniferous and broadleaf trees, the latter would have become dormant during the winter months and lost their leaves. Similarly, much of the ground vegetation would also have disappeared in the winter.

The Better to See You With

According to Anthony Fiorillo of the Dallas Museum of Natural History and Roland Gangloff of the University of Alaska Museum, *Troodon formosus* made its living, in part, with its very large eyes. This common theropod of northern climes was a small predatory biped measuring about 6 feet (1.8 m) long. It had proportionally one of the biggest brains of all dinosaurs and possibly high intelligence compared with

The North Slope of the Brooks Range, in modern Alaska, is colder now than it was in *Troodon's* time—but it was still relatively cold, and for much of the year, very dark.

FEATHERS FOR WARMTH

Another adaptation that may have helped some dinosaurs deal with the cold is an insulating layer of feathers. Recently, paleontologists have found evidence of feathers in several nonflying dinosaurs, leading to many speculations about the feathers' purpose. These dinosaurs include *Dilong*, a small tyrannosaurid; *Beipiaosaurus*, one of the largest feathered dinosaurs ever found at more than 7 feet (2.2 m) long; and *Sinornithosaurus*, a relative of *Velociraptor*. All three were discovered in China. Although no fossils from polar dinosaurs have yet shown the presence of feathers, some scientists believe the possibility cannot be discounted.

other dinosaurs. It also had a long head and jaws filled with small teeth, and strong hind limbs that likely provided good acceleration to help the lightweight, at 110–130 pounds (50–60 kg), dinosaur chase down its prey. Although the dinosaur was about the size of a man, its eyes were huge at 1.75 inches (4.4 cm) in diameter.

Fiorillo and Gangloff point out that *Troodon formosus* was one of the most common dinosaurs in Alaska, making up nearly 75 percent of all theropods that have been found there. This contrasts to southern parts of its range, including Alberta and Montana, where it was not as abundant as other similarly sized predator species, such as *Saurornitholestes langstoni*. In a paper published in the *Journal of Vertebrate Paleontology* in 2000, they stated, "We suggest that the reason why the North Slope fauna was dominated by a small theropod with exceptionally large eyes by hunting at night when its large eyes, again, would have been an advantage.

Australian Winters

On the opposite side of the globe, Australia was within the Antarctic Circle during the Cretaceous Period, and dinosaurs there also had to cope with cold and dark winters. One of the dinosaurs that many believe remained in the area year-round was *Leaellynasaura*, a small ornithopod that reached about 6.5 feet (2 m) as an adult. A cold-blooded animal living through the sub-zero winters would likely show a slowing or

(*Troodon formosus*) was because it was a taxon adapted for the low-light conditions of the high latitudes of its time." In southern regions where *Troodon* coexisted with *Saurornitholestes*, they speculate that *Saurornitholestes* may have been more competitive overall, but *Troodon* was still able to eke out a living

a halting of growth during the winter as its body temperature dropped, but *Leaellynasaura* fossils indicate that it continued to grow all year long. This may suggest that the dinosaur was warm-blooded, as was proposed by the two paleontologists who named the dinosaur.

This small, rapid predator lived across North America in the Late Cretaceous. *Troodon*, which means "wounding tooth," was named for its vicious teeth, of which it had more than 120 in its jaws.

CHAPTER 11

THE TRIALS OF BREEDING

THE REPRODUCTIVE AND PARENTING STRATEGIES of dinosaurs are little known. Although scientists can look to now-living birds and reptiles and make inferences about how dinosaurs courted and mated— and about whether the sometimes-massive animals cared for their young—the only hard evidence lies in the fossils. And this evidence is frequently less than conclusive.

Nonetheless, as paleontologists sift through an ever-expanding supply of skeletons, fossilized eggs, and trackways, they are beginning to form a clearer picture of dinosaur reproduction. A better understanding of ornaments on some adults suggests that males of certain species may have attracted females or scared off rival males with large horns, frills, or other decorations. Likewise, hollow head structures on some species may have been used as resonating chambers for courtship calls. Discoveries of eggs, eggshells, and nests provide clues about how the eggs were formed inside the females' bodies and how they were laid. Adult skeletons with nests suggest at least limited parental care, and the discovery of adult skeletons with those of juveniles indicates that care in some cases may have extended beyond hatching.

As fossil evidence mounts, scientists will no doubt continue to refine the picture of dinosaur reproduction.

Maiasaura dinosaurs, whose name means "good mother reptile," are so called because of fossil discoveries of huge nesting grounds. It is surmised that these dinosaurs, in addition to brooding in large herds, guarded and cared for their eggs and possibly their hatched offspring as well.

The Mating Game

Peacocks fan their tails, lightning bugs flash, jumping spiders dance, and nightingales sing to attract a mate. What did the dinosaurs do?

Trumpeting Call

If the sound emanating from the computers of scientists at Sandia National Laboratories and the New Mexico Museum of Natural History and Science is any indication, at least some dinosaur species produced a low-frequency rumble. The researchers analyzed a newly discovered skull of the hadrosaur *Parasaurolophus*, ran a bevy of calculations through powerful computers, and simulated the call

Although the purpose of such sounds is still a matter for conjecture, many speculate that the trumpeting calls were used to communicate and possibly for courtship. Supporting these speculations is the structure of fossilized *Parasaurolophus* ear bones, which suggests that the dinosaurs could hear low-pitched sounds.

Another hadrosaur suspected of making sounds is *Corythosaurus*. It also had a crest, although it was smaller than that of *Parasaurolophus*; this crest could have amplified the sounds it produced. Such sounds could also have been used for communication and courtship.

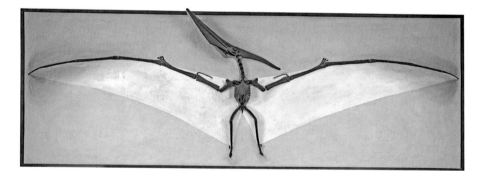

Pterosaur head crests may have been used in mating displays. It is possible that dinosaur head crests served similar purposes.

of that dinosaur in 1997, some 75–65 million years after it roamed the Earth. They and many other scientists believe the large, herbivorous *Parasaurolophus* likely used its 4.5- to 6-foot (1.4–1.8 m) head crest with its trumpetlike internal tubes to amplify sounds it produced.

Displays

Just as some lizards bob their heads or show off a colorful patch of skin, certain dinosaurs may have had displays of their own either for use during male-to-male confrontation or for attracting a mate at breeding time.

An example is *Dilophosaurus*, a 20-foot-long (6 m) bipedal theropod with a pair of thin, rounded, bony crests running forward along the snout and back past its eyes. Although the dinosaur did not have the expandable collar depicted in the movie *Jurassic Park*, its pair of head crests would have been quite suitable for display purposes and possibly used to entice a female to mate.

Other dinosaurs with features that may have been used in displays include *Allosaurus*, which had short brow horns, and *Citipati*, a birdlike dinosaur with a thin crest on its head, among others. Certain postures or movements, like head bobbing, would have made these features stand out, but the fossil record is limited in its ability to verify such behaviors.

Spiny Attraction

Another dinosaur that some speculate had a display feature is *Spinosaurus*. Ranging in size from 52–59 feet (16–18 m), the large-headed, bipedal theropod had long spines rising up to 6.5 feet (2 m) above its back. One interpretation is that the spines were covered with thin skin, forming a prominent sail, something like the fin of a fish. The sail may well have been used for display. The sail—or hump if it was more thickly covered with muscle—may have been networked with blood vessels, as some scientists have proposed, and could have helped to regulate internal body temperature.

It is possible that the distinctive head crest of *Parasaurolophus* amplified vocalizations, allowing it to make trumpeting calls to its offspring or its herd-mates.

Dinosaur Eggs

In 1859, Jean-Jacques Pouech, an amateur geologist, became the first modern human to find dinosaur eggs. The eggs were located near the Pyrenees in southern France; partly because Pouech misidentified them as large fossilized bird eggs, the discovery received little attention. Decades later, in 1923, Roy Chapman Andrews and a team from the American Museum of Natural History went to lands bordering China and Mongolia and uncovered egg

exact species of dinosaur to which they belonged was difficult or impossible; thus many of the fossil eggs were assigned only scientific names, so-called oogenus and oospecies, that described the fossils: *Spheroolithus irenensis* for the round eggs and *Elongatoolithus* species for the oval-shaped ones.

Newer Discoveries

Since Pouech's and the Andrews team's discoveries, dinosaur eggs

Identifying dinosaur eggs often consists solely of conjecture. This one may belong to a *Hypselosaurus*, a smaller, Late Cretaceous sauropod from Europe and a debated genus in itself.

fragments that they properly identified as those of a dinosaur. If they were whole, the eggs would have been a bit smaller than a softball. As with many other egg finds since, the determination of the

have been found in various locations, including Europe, Asia, North and South America, and Africa. Many of the fossil sites, sometimes with eggs numbering in the hundreds of thousands, were in mudstones—formations of unlayered sedimentary rock—along what were once floodplains. Apparently, the adults laid the eggs in the dry season, and both eggshells and unhatched eggs were covered when the following rainy season came and thereafter preserved for the ages.

Caudipteryx Twins

Dinosaur eggs are still drawing much attention. In 2005, for example, a research team led by Tamaki Sato of the Canadian Museum of Nature, announced that it had found eggs still inside the pelvis of a female *Caudipteryx*, a feathered, but nonflying theropod that measured about 10 feet (3 m) long. The team described

the elongate eggs as the same size: 6.7 inches (17 cm) long and nearly filling the female's pelvic cavity, no doubt soon to be laid. Based on the similar dimensions of the two eggs, the team hypothesized that the female had two oviducts and each simultaneously produced an egg. The finding might explain the paired groupings of eggs within some previously found multiple-egg nests of the closely related *Oviraptor*.

This dinosaur egg may be called *Spheroolithus irenensis*, a designation merely describing its spherical shape rather than its species.

Nests and Parental Care

Like reptiles and birds, many dinosaurs laid their eggs in nests. Over the past few decades, increasing interest among paleontologists is beginning to shed light not only on what the nests looked like, but also on whether the adults provided any parental care.

Size and Shape

Dinosaur nests vary. Some, like those of *Dendroolithus*, contain closely packed eggs. Those of *Maiasaura* (eggs named *Spheroolithus maiasauroides*) often contain fewer than a dozen eggs distributed in a ring; nests of *Protoceratopsidovum* eggs are ring-shaped, but the eggs—sometimes 20 or more—are grouped in pairs. Others, like *Megaloolithus* eggs from France, were laid in a far less organized manner: the female apparently dug a conical hole and simply laid them inside and departed.

Nests of dinosaur eggs varied from dinosaur to dinosaur. Some nests were tightly organized, but in others, eggs were laid in a more haphazard manner. Some nests were shallow holes in the ground; others were deep pits, containing successive layers of eggs, one on top of another.

Colony Nesting

Often, scientists discover several clutches of eggs in the same area. China, India, France, Mongolia, and the appropriately named Egg Mountain in Montana,

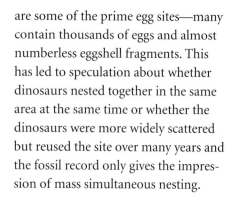

are some of the prime egg sites—many contain thousands of eggs and almost numberless eggshell fragments. This has led to speculation about whether dinosaurs nested together in the same area at the same time or whether the dinosaurs were more widely scattered but reused the site over many years and the fossil record only gives the impression of mass simultaneous nesting.

Parental Care

Parental care among dinosaurs is also a widely discussed topic. One of the dinosaurs with good evidence for this behavior is *Maiasaura*, some eggs of which have been discovered with embryos inside. Analyses of the eggs and embryos indicate that new hatchlings were altricial (essentially helpless) and unable to wander out from the nest or to survive on their own. A rough parallel from our time would be songbird hatchlings, which require significant and prolonged parental care. Although this is the prevailing opinion, it is not unanimous. Nicholas Geist and Terry Jones of Oregon State University contend that the hip bones in *Maiasaura* hatchlings are advanced enough to allow them to venture from the nest to find their own food.

An intriguing 2005 study provides support for the concept of parental care of the young in another species of dinosaur. A team led by Robert Reisz of the University of Toronto announced that fossil eggs found nearly three decades earlier in South Africa were those of *Massospondylus carinatus*, a herbivorous prosauropod dinosaur. Interestingly, the embryos preserved inside the eggs were not only well-developed and ready to hatch, but had no teeth or teeth so soft that they were not fossilized. The researchers believe this suggests that the newly hatched young would have been unable to feed on plants right away and would have required the assistance of a parent to survive.

Defending the Nest

For many dinosaurs, however, parental care may have extended no further than defending the eggs. Evidence of parental attention to the nest is fairly clear. Skeletons of adult *Oviraptors*, for example, have been found sitting atop clutches of eggs. The parents were probably not brooding the eggs as birds do, however. Studies of the number and the arrangement of the eggs and the size of the adult suggest that the adult could squat over and, likely with the help of its feathers, could warm some, but not all,

of the eggs. This would have left some out in the cold. Such a stance, however, can be interpreted as the adult merely guarding its eggs from predators rather than brooding them.

An *Oviraptor* skeleton atop its unhatched eggs. Initially believed to be an egg thief, scientists later concluded that the misunderstood *Oviraptor* was merely trying to incubate its own eggs.

STOP, THIEF!

For many years, *Oviraptor* got a bad rap that stemmed from the discovery of a nest of dinosaur eggs with the skeleton of an adult dinosaur on top. Scientists identified the adult as an *Oviraptor*, the nest as that of a *Protoceratops*, and concluded that the *Oviraptor* had preyed on the *Protoceratops* eggs. In fact, the name *Oviraptor* means "egg thief," and this particular species is *Philoceratops*, which means "an affinity for ceratopsians." Eventually, the nest was found to be that of the *Oviraptor*. Rather than being a nest raider, it was apparently simply being a good parent and guarding its own eggs.

PART 4

FOSSILS, FAME, AND FORTUNE

CHAPTER 12

EARLY RIVALRY

"DINOSAUR HUNTER"—a vividly colorful job description. For the uninitiated, it might conjure up a few days' hacking fossils out of the ground at a dig site, a short time cleaning and assembling the fossils into a beautifully complete skeleton of an exciting new dinosaur, and months of subsequent fame, media attention, press conferences, respect from fellow paleontologists, and adulation from the "monster-loving" public.

The reality, of course, is far from this glamorous, romanticized view. Searching for fossils of dinosaurs and other life-forms, assessing the initial finds, painstaking excavation, removing finds under difficult and sometimes dangerous working conditions, lengthy preparation and cleaning, careful scientific description, and, at last, publication, are all more characteristic of paleontologists' work.

Dinosaurs caught the public's attention in the mid-nineteenth century as massively monstrous long-gone beasts soon after the word *dinosaur* was coined. The first speculative, life-sized reconstructions were put on display in cities such as London and New York and fired the imagination. Soon waves of "dinosaur fever" were sweeping through Europe, North America, and beyond. Particularly in North America, scrambles ensued to find new fossils, bestow new names, break records, and generally outdo rivals. This culminated in the infamous "Bone Wars" of the late nineteenth century between Othniel Charles Marsh and Edward Drinker Cope.

Left: The Morrison Formation, seen here in Utah (with outcrops in other states), has been a popular destination for dinosaur hunters since the "Bone Wars" following a fossil discovery in 1877. Pages 154–155: Paleontologists work painstakingly to uncover a fossilized *Tyrannosaurus rex*.

Before the Dinosauria

Early dinosaurs walked the Earth more than 225 million years ago. Their rule over the land, as the biggest terrestrial herbivores and carnivores ever, lasted for 150 million years. These immense time spans contrast with the less than 200 years of scientific study of these great beasts.

Before the early 1800s, people were certainly interested in the fossils of dinosaurs and other animals and plants. They examined, collected, and even worshipped these strangely shaped pieces of stone. But they lacked the scientific techniques and knowledge to make sense of the fossils. They also lived at a time when religious beliefs tended to shape scientific reasoning, and when misconceptions, if repeated often and convincingly enough, grew to be seen as the scientific truth.

Gradually, fossil discoveries and descriptions stimulated more scientific debate about the nature and origins of these curious items. Fossils also became fashionably collectible. The rich and famous gathered decorative fossils and spectacular shells, pinned insects, pressed flowers, and displayed stuffed birds in their home museums of "nature's treasury."

An early illustration of *Mosasaurus* fossils from 1866. The first mosasaur to be discovered, in a mine in the 1770s, *Mosasaurus* was at the forefront of early interest in fossil hunting.

> "All of these facts, consistent among themselves, and not opposed by any report, seem to me to prove the existence of a world previous to ours, destroyed by some kind of catastrophe."
>
> —BARON GEORGES CUVIER, 1796, CONCERNING THE ANATOMY OF FOSSIL AND LIVING ELEPHANTS

Shifting Opinions

During the early nineteenth century, the explanations given for fossils began to shift from proposals that they were shaped by the natural forces of wind, water, and weather, or fashioned by gods, spirits, or magical powers. More evidence-based views began to take hold. More and more, people began to view fossils as the preserved remains of dead animals and plants.

A leading figure in this transition was Georges Cuvier (1769–1832). One of Europe's most respected scientists, Cuvier was for many years professor of animal anatomy at the National Museum of Natural History in Paris, France. He was instrumental in founding the scientific disciplines of vertebrate paleontology and comparative anatomy, viewing each organism as a functionally integrated whole and comparing bodily structures and functions across the animal kingdom. The French nation bestowed many honors upon him, making him a French state councilor and baron and naming him a peer of the realm.

Extinction

The concept of evolution was not part of Cuvier's scientific vocabulary (Charles Darwin's famous book *On the Origin of Species by Means of Natural Selection* was not published until 27 years after Cuvier's death). He did, however, help to change the views of his day about extinctions. Many of Cuvier's contemporaries accepted that fossils were the remains of once-living organisms. But many also believed that such organisms were still extant, surviving somewhere in the world, unknown to science, rather than having become extinct. Cuvier suggested that the Earth had suffered from periodic disasters or catastrophes, such as massive floods, which he termed "revolutions." At these times, Cuvier maintained, various life forms perished, with new ones appearing, ready-made, to repopulate the land and sea. This had happened several times, according to Cuvier, thus explaining the fossil record in the rocks.

Cuvier thus helped gain scientific acceptance for the idea of extinction, which was a necessary step for the "reappearance" of the long-gone dinosaurs.

A marble bust of Georges Cuvier, by David d'Angers, 1833. Cuvier's ideas about extinction helped to propel scientific understanding of the history of life on Earth.

Important Teeth

The first dinosaur to be given an official scientific name was not actually known as a *dinosaur*—that term did not yet exist. As described earlier, *Megalosaurus* was named in 1824 by William Buckland, based on a fossil jaw and teeth found in a quarry at Stonesfield, near Oxford, England, in about 1815.

time to explore the surrounding South Downs and Weald, where the rocks are mainly chalk-based marine sediments from the Late Cretaceous Period. His collections of fossils, rocks, and other specimens were displayed, as was the fashion of the time, in his home museum. Mantell was an eminent geologist; he wrote *The Fossils of the South Downs* (1822)—a book praised by King George IV.

Iguanodon earned its name from the similarity between its teeth and those of an iguana. The rest of the early descriptions of Iguanodon have been superseded by more modern science, but the name has stuck.

The following year, 1825, saw the second dinosaur to be given a name: the large ornithopod *Iguanodon*. Gideon Mantell (1790–1852), a well-known collector of rocks and fossils in England, gave this dinosaur its appellation. Mantell, a physician based in Lewes, in the southern county of Sussex, used his spare

A Large Lizard

Many of Mantell's finds came from quarries, pits, mines, and road cuttings. The story goes that around 1822 his wife Mary discovered some fossil teeth in a roadside pile of gravel. (A monument unveiled in 2000 at Whiteman's Green, Cuckfield, West Sussex, now marks the approximate site of this historic find.) Mantell was fascinated by the extraordinary size and peculiar shape of the teeth. He showed them to various experts, who said they were relatively recent and could be from a big fish. Richard Owen, who would coin the name *Dinosauria* some 20 years later, opined that they were mammalian. Georges Cuvier suggested they might have belonged to a recently dead rhinoceros. However, apparently Cuvier ventured this opinion late at night, after a celebration, and the next day changed his mind.

Mantell suspected that the teeth were much older and of Mesozoic origin. During a visit to London, he noted that they were similar in shape to the teeth of the iguana lizard, although some 20 times larger. He decided to name the find and toyed with *Iguanosaurus*. But fellow geologist William Daniel Conybeare pointed out that such a name could equally apply to the living iguana lizard and made no reference to the teeth. Accordingly, in his 1825 report, Mantell suggested that the teeth came from a huge, extinct, plant-eating lizard perhaps 60 feet (18 m) long, which he named *Iguanodon*, "iguana tooth."

Tragic End

In 1833, Mantell described and named a third ancient reptile that would be included in the dinosaur group. This was the armored *Hylaeosaurus*, "woodland lizard," an ankylosaur. Its fossils came from the Tilgate Forest area of Sussex, a place he frequented in his fieldwork. From this time, Mantell suffered a series of tragedies. Rivals in the scientific establishment, led by Richard Owen, belittled him. His medical practice went bankrupt and he was forced to sell his treasured fossil and rock collections to the British Museum. His wife left him, his son Walter moved to New Zealand, and his daughter Hannah died. Having moved to London, he suffered a terrible back injury in a carriage accident and developed scoliosis, a painful spinal deformity. He took to opium as a painkiller and finally, lonely and overlooked, died from an overdose of that drug.

Gideon Mantell, who named *Iguanodon* in 1825 and proposed an "Age of Reptiles" in 1831.

The Dinosaurs Are Born

Dinosaurs first appeared more than 200 million years ago—and also, in a manner of speaking, less than 200 years ago. The word *Dinosauria* was coined in 1841–42 by eminent English anatomist Richard Owen (1804–92) for what he called "a distinct tribe or suborder of saurian reptiles." Owen used ancient Greek for the name, with *deinos* usually interpreted as "terrible," but in the sense of "formidable" or "awesome" rather than "frightful" or "awful," and *saura/ sauros* as "lizard," or sometimes "reptile."

The Natural History Museum in London has as imposing a place in the history of paleontology as its façade has in the city's landscape. It opened its doors to a public curious about the new dinosaurs in 1881.

The stimulus for creating this new grouping of extinct reptiles was Owen's study of various fossils, including those of *Megalosaurus*, *Iguanodon*, and *Hylaeosaurus*. Owen was impressed by their size and majesty and also by various anatomical features that, he concluded, merited a separate grouping. They were not types of lizards or crocodiles—in fact, they were unlike any living reptiles. So he decided that *Megalosaurus*, *Iguanodon*, and *Hylaeosaurus* deserved their own category. Thus the word *dinosaur* came into being, with the aforementioned genera as the three founding members of the group.

Owen's Legacy

At the time of naming the Dinosauria, Owen was Hunterian professor at London's Royal College of Surgeons and spent much time cataloguing and describing its collections. His reputation as an anatomist and fossil expert was growing steadily, following publication of articles on a wide array of living and extinct animals. His subjects ranged from the shellfish known as brachiopods, or lampshells, to the pearly nautilus (a cousin of octopus and squid), to wormlike parasites of human muscle.

In 1856, Owen was named superintendent of the Natural History department of the British Museum, located in central London. He worked tirelessly to raise both the profile of the natural sciences and his department's status to that of an independent museum housed in a separate building. After much planning and maneuvering, by the early 1880s the British Museum (Natural History) had separated from the main British Museum site. Owen supervised the relocation of its collections, including by now several more dinosaurs, to a huge new building (it opened 1881) in west London. Today, the since-renamed Natural History Museum still occupies the building and is one of the world's centers for collections, expedition-organizing, research, and display, not only of dinosaurs but

the whole range of extant and extinct animal and plant life.

Owen continued to publish prolifically, and his *Comparative Anatomy and Physiology of Vertebrates* (completed 1868) achieved great renown, as did his *History of British Fossil Reptiles* (completed 1884).

A man of considerable talent but questionable charm, Richard Owen is perhaps best remembered for his use of the term *dinosaur*, which he coined in 1841.

CONTROVERSIAL FELLOW

Richard Owen, who coined the word *dinosaur*, was a complex character who was heartily disliked by certain of his contemporaries. His personality and career—and his methods of befriending the rich, influential, and important—were controversial. He tended to take credit for work that was not his, and he was accused not only of plagiarism, which led to his dismissal from the councils of the Royal Society and Zoological Society, but of slandering or making false accusations against fellow scientists. These rivals included Gideon Mantell; Owen claimed for himself the discovery of *Iguanodon* and several other Mantell finds. Mantell referred to him as "dastardly and envious," and an Oxford professor remarked that he "lied for God and for malice."

Dinomania!

Dinosaurs did not remain a back-water of scientific curiosity for long. During the 1840s, news of recently discovered fossils that represented huge, fearsome reptiles from the past was filtering through to the general public in Britain. People clamored to know more about these great beasts, how big and fierce they were, and what they might have looked like when alive.

Palace—was constructed to house the major displays and exhibits. After the exhibition, the building was dismantled and moved to Sydenham in southeast London. At the time, dinosaurs were big news. Richard Owen, who—as described—was the coiner of the word *dinosaur* and a leading authority on them, was asked to arrange for models of dinosaurs and other great extinct creatures, to be built to actual size as in life, for the Crystal Palace gardens. These would be the world's first life-like, life-sized dinosaur reconstructions—and, in effect, the first-ever "dinosaur theme park."

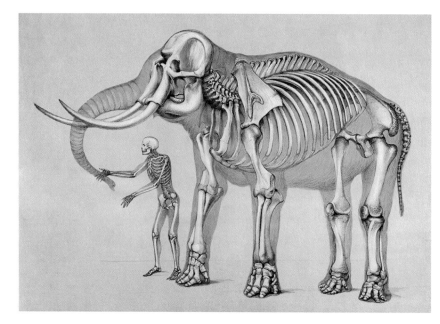

A talented artist, Benjamin Waterhouse Hawkins's comparison of an elephant and a human showcases his anatomical knowledge, which was put to great effect in the dinosaur sculptures of the Great Exhibition.

In 1850–51, the Great Exhibition was held in Hyde Park, central London. Its primary aim was to celebrate the indus-trial, economic, and military success of Great Britain and its vast empire. A giant new building with an iron skel-eton, clad in acres of glass—the Crystal

Array of Animals

Between 1852 and 1854 Owen worked with the sculptor Benjamin Waterhouse Hawkins to make these huge models. They included not only dinosaurs such as *Iguanodon*, *Hylaeosaurus*, and *Megalosaurus*, but also assorted flying pterosaurs, swimming ichthyosaurs and mosasaurs, mammals including the giant ground sloth *Megatherium* and the "Irish giant elk" *Megaloceros*, and some large amphibianlike creatures known as labyrinthodonts. To modern eyes, the dinosaurs especially are very different from the way they are reconstructed and portrayed today. *Iguanodon* was shown on all fours with limbs angled out to the sides, like a typical lizard, rather than in the dinosaurian upright stance. Owen and his colleagues had extremely limited knowledge of the dinosaurs, since only a very few fossils of a very few kinds were then known.

An 1886 engraving by Cornelius Brown of the Crystal Palace. Built specifically for the Great Exhibition of 1851, it was destroyed in 1936 by a fire.

Dinosaur Dinner

On New Year's Eve 1853, Hawkins and Owen organized a dinner party, partly to celebrate their models but also as a publicity stunt. About 20 fossil experts were invited, including William Buckland, Georges Cuvier, and even Gideon Mantell. The gathering ate their meal within the mold used to create the life-sized body of *Iguanodon*.

When the dinosaurs and other models were put on show at Crystal Palace, they created a sensation. People flocked to gaze at them open-mouthed in awe. The first phase of "dinosaur fever" had begun. A wave of fossil hunting began as people started scouring the countryside, looking for fossils of dinosaurs and other huge, long-gone creatures.

As more dinosaurs were discovered, the accuracy of the Crystal Palace models was called into question. By the end of the nineteenth century, they and their gardens had fallen into disrepute and disrepair. The glass building of the Crystal Palace was infamously destroyed by fire in 1936. But the dinosaurs and other models have recently been repaired, renovated, and replaced as necessary, to their original condition and position. They are part of a display of historical interest at Crystal Palace Park, along with exhibits covering 350 million years of British geology. They remain a great attraction.

Deep in a Coal Mine

An old-fashioned construction of an *Iguanodon* skeleton, with an upright, kangaroolike stance.

During the middle of the nineteenth century, news of dinosaurs and their fossils spread out from Britain, across Europe, and over to North America. Dinosaur fever received a great boost from a marvelous discovery in March 1878 in Belgium. In the village of Bernissart, some 1,050 feet (320 m) below the surface in the Sainte Barbe coal mine, workers discovered a "mass grave" of dinosaurian and other fossils. The remains had accumulated in a clay-filled crack that ran across the coal seam being worked. They were found by two miners, Jules Créteur and Alphonse Blanchard, who thought they had discovered fragments of petrified wood infiltrated by gold. Further study showed the pieces were fossil animal bones filled with iron pyrites ("fool's gold," a natural iron sulfate).

Excavation work was supervised by Louis de Pauw and the Royal Museum of Natural History in Brussels (now Belgium's Royal Institute of Natural Sciences). Eventually they extracted the remains of more than 30 *Iguanodon*, some with just a few parts but others almost complete skeletons. Fossils of crocodiles, turtles, fish, and plants were also found at the site. As each skeleton was uncovered, detailed notes and drawings were made of its position, and it was coded for identification. The fossils were transported by mine wagons and elevator to the surface, then by rail to Brussels. Removing the remains took about three years.

Iguanodon Stands Tall

At the museum, the best-preserved, most complete skeletons were chosen for reconstruction of *Iguanodon* as it would have appeared in life. Belgian fossil expert Louis Dollo (1857–91) oversaw this phase of the work, assisted by de Pauw. Dollo's report of 1882 described how the fossils had been excavated and reassembled. His reconstruction showed *Iguanodon* in an almost upright pose, similar to a kangaroo. In fact, Dollo used as reference the skeletons of modern animals such as kangaroos, wallabies, and emus to help rebuild *Iguanodon*. The upright stance correlated with the earlier ideas of Joseph Leidy in the United States, rather than with the proposals of Owen and others in England. Today, *Iguanodon* is usually reconstructed with its body leaning forward, neck stretched in front and tail behind, and its four limbs directly below the body.

Bernissart's fossil *Iguanodon* skeletons went on display in 1883 at the Royal Institute of Natural Sciences in Parc Leopold, Brussels. Some were reconstructed in the upright posture described above and grouped together as though traveling as a herd. Other remains were arranged to recreate their original positions when discovered in the mine.

The original fossils had received careful conservation, but they began to deteriorate because of contact with the air and the varying temperatures in the museum. In 1932, the sad state of the displays made headlines in Belgium and beyond. Eventually the decision was made to dismantle the reconstructions into individual items—more than 1,200 of them. Over several months during 1935–36, the fossils were treated in a special consolidating solution. The displays were then reassembled within enormous temperature- and humidity-controlled glass cabinets.

The dentition of *Iguanodon* was designed to allow the dinosaur to grind down its plant food with its long, ridged cheek teeth.

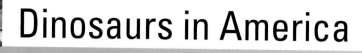

Dinosaurs in America

Early waves of "dinomania" in Britain and Europe had parallels in North America. The size and monstrous appearance of the dinosaurs, and the publicity generated by Hawkins's life-sized models at London's Crystal Palace sparked the interest of the American public. One of the first U.S. paleontologists was Joseph Leidy (1823–91). Leidy, known as the founder of vertebrate paleontology in North America, gained fame and respect as a comparative anatomist, professor of anatomy at the University of Pennsylvania, noted parasitologist, student of human biology, avid supporter of the use of microscopes in science, and an accomplished scientific illustrator. Beginning in 1850 and continuing through the late 1860s, Leidy collaborated with the Smithsonian Institution in the study of its fossil collections.

In the mid-1850s, Leidy named several dinosaurs from newly discovered fossils, although these specimens were very limited and fragmentary, mostly teeth. They included the small, slim, fast meat-eater *Troodon*, which he named from a single tooth—at the

Above: Joseph Leidy (1823–91), one of America's earliest paleontologists.

Right: *Troodon*, by now one of the best known dinosaurs, was first named by Joseph Leidy in 1856.

time, he suspected it might have been a lizard; the bigger carnivore *Deinodon*, which was similar to the English *Megalosaurus*; and the large duckbilled herbivore *Trachodon*, which Leidy compared to *Iguanodon*.

Clues from a Quarry

In 1858, Joseph Leidy had the opportunity to study a major new find of

William Parker Foulke (1816–65). The latter man had traced the origins of large fossil bones that had been found 20 years earlier in a quarry in Haddonfield, New Jersey. He relocated the abandoned quarry, which was overgrown and partly filled. Foulke and his team began their excavations and unearthed fossils of a huge creature, including teeth, vertebrae, and bones from the front and rear limbs. Foulke sent the specimens to Leidy, who noted their resemblance to *Iguanodon* fossils from England. The result was the large duckbilled dinosaur *Hadrosaurus*. This was not only the first relatively complete dinosaur skeleton found in the United States, but also the most complete dinosaur skeleton known at the time.

Ten years later, in 1868, the reconstructed skeleton of *Hadrosaurus* was displayed at the Philadelphia Academy of Natural Sciences, where it still stands—though it is now positioned in a horizontal pose, rather than its initial upright, bipedal, kangaroolike pose (which contrasted sharply with the all-fours, sprawling reconstructions of *Iguanodon* in England). In 1991, New Jersey adopted *Hadrosaurus* as its official state dinosaur. However, its remains are similar to many other hadrosaurs, making it difficult to support *Hadrosaurus* as a distinctive genus.

DINOSAURS IN CENTRAL PARK

Following the success of the Crystal Palace models in England, New York City decided to grab a piece of dinosaur action. In 1868, dinosaurs arrived in Central Park courtesy of the sculptor Benjamin Waterhouse Hawkins, who had masterminded the Crystal Palace displays. The life-sized models included *Hadrosaurus* and the 20-foot-long (6 m) theropod *Laelaps*, probably an early tyrannosaur, whose fossils had been found by Edward Drinker Cope. It transpired that the name *Laelaps* was already in use for a species of mite, so in 1877 it was changed to *Dryptosaurus*.

A *Prosaurolophus* displayed in a near-horizontal pose. Originally thought to stand upright, it is now believed that hadrosaurs regularly walked closer to the ground, occasionally on all fours.

Bone Wars

The last quarter of nineteenth-century paleontology was dominated by two famous American personalities, Othniel Charles Marsh (1831–99) and Edward Drinker Cope (1840–97). Their heated rivalry has become legend and is usually referred to as the "Bone Wars."

Marsh was a Yale graduate who studied in Europe for several years, then returned in 1866 to become Yale's professor of vertebrate paleontology. He was instrumental in helping to establish the Peabody Museum of Natural History—its founder, George Peabody, was Marsh's uncle. In 1881, Marsh was appointed honorary curator of the Smithsonian's Department of Vertebrate Fossils.

Cope showed an interest in natural history from an early age, and became a member of the Megatherium Club, an influential group based at the Smithsonian Institution during the 1850s–60s. In 1867, he began his official collaboration with the Smithsonian. Like Marsh, he worked in Europe; he then took a series of U.S. appointments, including curator at the Academy of Natural Sciences in Philadelphia, professor of natural science at Haverford College in Pennsylvania, and professor of geology and paleontology at the University of Pennsylvania.

Othniel Charles Marsh (above) and Edward Drinker Cope (below) are better known for their vitriolic competition for fossil discovery than any particular fossil find.

A Rush for Fossils

In 1877, a North American "dinosaur rush" developed following the discovery of two rich fossil sites in Colorado. One near Cañon City was discovered by O. W. Lucas, a school teacher and part-time fossil hunter. He contacted Cope, who arranged the excavations. The other site was near Morrison, Colorado, and was discovered by Arthur Lakes—like Lucas, a teacher and fossil enthusiast. Lakes contacted Marsh, who organized a team to recover the fossils.

Marsh and Cope were already great rivals. They had first encountered each other in Berlin, Germany. In the United States, they had worked together briefly, locating fossils in the Connecticut Valley. However, Cope accused Marsh of bribing the local quarry managers to give Marsh first pick of the fresh finds. In about 1869, Cope had described the fossil skeleton of the sea reptile *Elasmosaurus*, a type of plesiosaur. Marsh saw that Cope had put the head at the wrong end—on the tip of the tail—and pointed it out to Cope, leading to an argument between the two. The dispute was eventually mediated

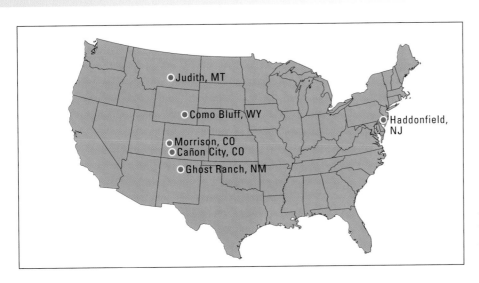

The dig sites of the "Bone Wars" spread out all over the American West.

by Joseph Leidy, who affirmed Marsh's appraisal, and spread the word about Cope's mistake. The incident further soured the relationship between Marsh and Cope.

Wild West Feud

By 1880, the rival teams of Marsh and Cope had spread their digs to sites in Montana, Wyoming, and New Mexico. Their feuding grew to extraordinary proportions. Members of one team would spy on the others, sabotage their excavations, plant misleading fossils from other sites, and disrupt their supplies of food and water. Sites were dynamited to prevent others continuing excavation, and Cope even hijacked a train carrying Marsh's fossils.

During this fevered period, both Cope and Marsh rushed to describe and name more dinosaurs and other vertebrates than one another. During the 1880s–90s, the two men coined more than 130 new dinosaur names between them, as well as describing and naming hundreds of other fossilized creatures. Some of this work was done in a hurry and certainly not to the exacting standards of today's paleontology, so certain of those names are no longer considered accurate. Cope's discoveries included the sauropod *Camarasaurus*, the slim theropod *Coelophysis*, and the *Triceratops*-like *Monoclonius*. Marsh's naming legacy encompasses *Triceratops*, *Stegosaurus*, the sauropods *Diplodocus* and *Apatosaurus*, and the huge meat-eater *Allosaurus*. The rivals died within two years of each other, and a semblance of calm then returned to American vertebrate paleontology.

Colorful Character

One of the most colorful and fascinating of all paleontologists was Baron Franz Nopcsa von Felső-Szilvás (1877–1933).

Born into a wealthy family of Hungarian aristocrats, Nopcsa (sometimes spelled Nopsca) became interested in dinosaurs after fossils were discovered in 1895 on land belonging to his sister, Ilona. He entered the University of Vienna to study paleontology and geology—interests that would become a central thread is his remarkably complex and varied life.

Nopcsa worked in the field and the laboratory, unearthing and studying dinosaurs from Transylvania, then part of the Austro-Hungarian Empire and now in northwest Romania. He found remains of sauropods and other groups; among the names he bestowed were *Doryphorosaurus, Paranthodon, Rhodanosaurus, Scolosaurus, Teinurosaurus,* and *Telmatosaurus*—however, many of these have been superseded or are no longer considered valid.

As a dinosaur scientist, Nopcsa was ahead of his time in several respects. During a period when the main preoccupation was rebuilding skeletons, he was one of the first paleontologists to speculate on the living dinosaur and how its physiology, muscles, heart and digestive system might have worked. Thus, he is considered to be a founder of paleobiology. In the area of nonavian Mesozoic dinosaurs, Nopcsa suggested that some types might have exhibited complex behaviors such as social interactions and parental care. He proposed that certain dinosaurs might have been warm-blooded or at least have had physiological mechanisms to maintain body temperature. Nopcsa also mused that birds might have evolved from fast-running dinosaurs that developed feathers. All of these topics have been discussed at length in recent years.

A Passion for Albania

Nopcsa was far from a shy, retiring paleontologist, geologist, and biologist.

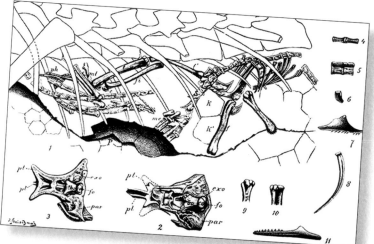

Above: An illustration of a *Compsognathus* fossil and the contents of its stomach by Baron Nopcsa, 1903.

Opposite, top: Baron Nopcsa, one of history's most eccentric paleontologists.

Opposite, bottom: Better known for their associations with creatures of fiction like vampires and werewolves, the Carpathian Mountains of Transylvania have yielded a number of dinosaur fossils.

He was deeply interested in Albania, then a province of the Ottoman Empire. He visited the region, traveled through its mountains, learned its languages and customs, and worked tirelessly for its independence. When independence was finally won, Nopcsa had high hopes of being the country's first leader. But he would never become King Nopcsa. President Ahmet Zogu took power in 1925, and in 1928 he declared himself King Zog I.

During World War I, Nopcsa worked as a spy for Austria-Hungary. After the war he moved to Vienna, but ran into financial trouble and was forced to sell his geological and paleontological collections to the British Museum (Natural History). In the end, he took his own life—first shooting his male secretary and long-standing companion and then himself.

REMEMBERED IN NAME

In 1913, fragmentary dinosaurlike remains found in Romania were named *Elopteryx*, "small wing." The full species was given the name of *Elopteryx nopcsai*, in honor of Baron Franz Nopcsa. The fossils may be from a small theropod, perhaps a maniraptoran or "raptor." They are so limited, however, that a firm identification is not possible, and the status of *Elopteryx* is usually considered as *nomen dubium* ("doubtful name").

CHAPTER 13

DIFFICULT AND DANGEROUS WORK

AS THE NINETEENTH CENTURY turned into the twentieth, fossil hunting was in good shape, especially in North America. Famous names such as Barnum Brown and the Sternbergs excavated the inhospitable "Badlands" of the continent's west-central regions. Tremendous discoveries were made, including *Tyrannosaurus* and its smaller cousin *Albertosaurus*. But the work was often difficult, done in harsh surroundings and Spartan conditions.

Fossil hunters were busy elsewhere on the globe, venturing into very different regions—including the tropical swamp-surrounded quarries of East Africa, the vast Sahara Desert of North Africa, the crags and caves of South Africa, and the bleak, windswept grasslands and rocky-sandy deserts of Asia, especially the Gobi of Mongolia. Here was uncovered the first good evidence for dinosaur nests and eggs. In the 1920s, exciting fossils were also being unearthed in China. Notable discoveries of this time included the remains, not only of dinosaurs, but also of long-gone types of humans and their close relatives, which received popular names such as "Peking Man" (1923; Beijing, China) and "Taung child" (1925; North West Province, South Africa). Loose reporting and speculation led many to believe that humans and Mesozoic dinosaurs coexisted, an impression fostered by a spate of early "monster movies" such as *The Lost World* (1925), which was based on the 1912 novel by Sir Arthur Conan Doyle, and *King Kong* (1933), in which the great ape battles dinosaurs.

No one said it would be easy: Deep in the unforgiving Gobi Desert, astonishing dinosaur fossils can be found among the burning sands and parched plants. Parts of the Gobi would have looked similarly parched in the Mesozoic Era, though much of it was warm, wet, and verdant. The desert conditions, while unappealing for humans, are ideal for preserving fossils.

Barnum Brown

The first complete *Tyrannosaurus rex* skull was uncovered by Barnum Brown in 1908, and can still be seen on display at the American Museum of Natural History.

A leading figure in North American pale-ontology during the late nineteenth and a good part of the twenti-eth century was Barnum Brown (1879–1968). Well-organized, energetic, widely traveled, and suc-cessful, for most of his working life Brown was employed as the curator of the American Museum of Natural History in New York. He worked tirelessly not only as a field surveyor, prospector, and collector, but also an as "acquirer" of fossils, some-times agreeing to buy for the museum a find that he had not actually seen.

Brown took his first fossil-finding trip in 1894 under the supervision of U.S. paleon-tologist Samuel Wendell Williston (1851–1918), professor of geol-ogy and anatomy at the University of Kansas. In 1897, Brown joined the museum and worked in Wyoming, arranging for the excava-tion of more than 60 tons of fossils. In 1902 came one of his greatest achieve-ments, the discovery of fossils at Hell Creek, Montana; Henry Fairfield Osborn subsequently named these fos-sils *Tyrannosaurus rex*. As mentioned earlier, Brown also found a second, more complete *Tyrannosaurus* in 1908.

Floating Base

From about 1910, Brown became interested in the fossils along the Red Deer River near Drumheller, Alberta, Canada. Wheeled vehicles were useless in such rocky, hilly country, so Brown

Tyrannosaurus rex, the king of the Late Cretaceous right up until the K/T mass extinc-tion, became king again for a time following its discovery.

Hell Creek, MT

"Brown . . . is the best man in the field that I ever had. He is very energetic, has great powers of endurance, walking thirty miles a day without fatigue, is very methodical in all his habits, and thoroughly honest."

—U.S. PALEONTOLOGIST SAMUEL WENDELL WILLISTON, 1895

arranged for a large barge to travel along the Red Deer River, acting as floating "base camp" for his teams of collectors. Brown's discoveries included the horned plant-eaters *Anchiceratops* and *Leptoceratops*, the duckbilled dinosaurs, or hadrosaurs, *Corythosaurus*, *Kritosaurus*, and *Saurolophus*, and the "bone-head" *Pachycephalosaurus*.

In the 1980s, Canadian paleontologist Phil Currie, formerly head of Dinosaur Research at the Royal Tyrrell Museum of Paleontology in Drumheller, restudied some fossils found by Brown, including those of *Albertosaurus*. Currie decided that the original find site might prove fruitful and used an old photograph to find it in Dry Island Buffalo Jump Provincial Park. Excavations opened again in 1988 and continued until 2005 under the supervision of Currie. In 2006, after becoming a chair at the Biological Sciences Department at the University of Alberta, Currie resumed excavations at the site.

Beautiful but unwelcoming landscape surrounds Red Deer River, whose rocky banks clearly show rock striations—visual markers of geologic time.

Brown's parents apparently named him "Barnum" after the flamboyant U.S. showman of the time, Phineas T. Barnum. Like the original Barnum, Brown was a celebrated personality. He frequented excavations dressed in a long fur coat and was a noted ballroom dancer. For work and pleasure, he did not limit himself to North America. He traveled to South America, northeast Africa, and India. Brown always had a keen eye for fruitful collaboration and sponsorship, and he developed a relationship with the Sinclair Oil Company. In return for funding, Brown wrote booklets about dinosaurs and fossils for the company and also kept a lookout for possible mineral-rich sites. He was involved with the dinosaur exhibits at the world's fairs in Chicago in the 1930s and New York in the 1960s.

Barnum Brown, in 1914, dressed in his characteristic fur coat while examining fossils on site.

Red Deer River

The Royal Tyrrell Museum of Paleontology, named after paleontologist Joseph Tyrrell, is surrounded by Alberta's fossil-rich badlands.

From the 1880s, North American dinosaur hunters started to prospect at various sites in Canada. In 1884, a fine fossil skull of a fearsome-looking meat-eating dinosaur was found in the Red Deer River Valley, Alberta. Discovered by Joseph Tyrrell (1858–1957), who was working for the Geological Survey of Canada, the remains were initially identified by Edward Drinker Cope as a specimen of the carnivore *Laelaps* (now *Dryptosaurus*). In 1905, however, Henry Fairfield Osborn, of the American Museum of Natural History, decided that they were distinct enough to be recognized as a different genus. He bestowed the name *Albertosaurus*, after the Canadian province where the specimens were found. In fact, Alberta itself had also just been officially named, on September 1, 1905, after the fourth daughter of Britain's Queen Victoria, Princess Louise Caroline Alberta. She was married to the Marquess of Lorne, governor general of Canada from 1878 to 1883. So

A river runs through it: The badlands surrounding Red Deer River are lucrative for paleontologists.

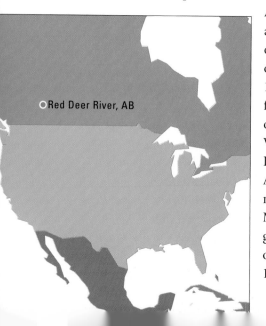

Red Deer River, AB

Albertosaurus is one of the few dinosaurs named, in effect, after a princess.

Joseph Tyrrell was not especially dedicated to dinosaur paleontology. From about 1898, he traveled widely and was involved in various gold, coal, and other mining projects from Ontario to the Klondike Arctic. Eventually he made a fortune from Ontario's gold mines. He received a number of awards, including medals from the Royal Society of Canada and the Geological Society of London. In 1985, he was honored by having the Royal Tyrrell Museum of Paleontology in Drumheller, Alberta, named for him. This museum has marvelous dinosaur fossils and displays, including horned dinosaurs, or ceratopsians, such as *Centrosaurus*, and duckbills, or hadrosaurs, such as *Lambeosaurus*.

Fossil-hunting Family

The Red Deer River during the mid-1910s was a magnet for fossil hunters.

In 1912, the Sternberg family—Charles H., George, Charles M., and Levi—began a series of expeditions, using a floating barge as their base, in a manner similar to Barnum Brown. The Sternbergs and Brown actually explored the area at the same time, and both sets of collectors scored many successes. Charles Hazelius Sternberg (1850–1943), who had worked with Edward Drinker Cope in Kansas, advanced the techniques of protecting delicate, crumbling fossils in cases or jackets of plaster and other substances. His book, *Hunting Dinosaurs in the Badlands of the Red Deer River* (1917), describes the hardships, difficult conditions, and days of fruitless digging compensated for by exciting finds.

Charles H's three sons all worked in vertebrate paleontology. George (1883–1969) is noted for his discovery of a 15-foot (4.6 m) specimen of the large Cretaceous fish *Xiphactinus*. This contained another fish, a 6-foot (1.8 m) *Gillicus*, inside it—presumably just swallowed—and has become known as the "fish within a fish." Charles Mortram (1885–1981) described and named several well-known dinosaurs, including the hulking, armored nodosaur *Edmontonia* (1928), the hypsilophodont-like *Parksosaurus* (1937), and the ceratopsian, or horned, dinosaur *Pachyrhinosaurus* (1950). Levi (1894–1976) developed techniques for copying fossils using latex casts. The elder Charles helped to found Calgary Zoo. Fossils collected by the Sternbergs, in particular George, are displayed at the Sternberg Museum of Natural History at Fort Hays State University, Kansas—home of the "fish within a fish."

One of Charles H. Sternberg's more remarkable finds, this "mummified" *Edmontosaurus* dinosaur has fossilized skin impressions.

Into Africa

In the early twentieth century, Africa began to yield notable dinosaur fossils. The most spectacular came from the Mtwara region of German East Africa, most of which is now Tanzania. From about 1907, an amazing series of massive remains were found in quarries known as Tendaguru. The first discoveries were brought to the attention of German geologist and paleontologist Eberhard Fraas (1862–1915), who, at the time, was searching for valuable minerals in the region. In 1913, Fraas named the small theropod *Procompsognathus*, probably a relation of *Coelophysis*; over the course of his life, he named other extinct vertebrates.

Within a year of the first finds at Tendaguru, German paleontologists Edwin Hennig (1882–1977) and Werner Janensch (1878–1969), from the Museum für Naturkunde (Museum of Natural History), Berlin, organized a complex expedition. The first series of excavations lasted about four years—to 1912. They yielded remains of the gigantic sauropod *Brachiosaurus*, the smaller diplodocidlike *Dicraeosaurus*, and the stegosaur-like *Kentrosaurus*. *Brachiosaurus* was already known from fossils found in Grand River Valley, Colorado, but the Tendaguru finds were more numerous and complete.

Difficult Conditions

In some respects, the rocks at Tendaguru can be compared with the Morrison Formation of the western United States. In Late Jurassic times, the Tendaguru region was a warm coastal plain, affected by occasional droughts. But in the early 1900s, it presented extremely difficult working conditions. Comforts were few, the heat and humidity stifling, the plagues of biting insects nearly intolerable, and the risk of contracting tropical diseases ever present. In Europe and North America, heavy loads of fossils were often transported by rail. With few roads and no railways in the region, the massive fossils of *Brachiosaurus* and others were split into pieces and carried by local porters more than 40 miles (65 km) to the port of Lindi. Over the four years, more than 250 tons of fossils were dug from Tendaguru and shipped to Berlin for study.

Giant Skeleton

Back in Berlin, the *Brachiosaurus* finds were cleaned from their surrounding matrix and pieced back together in the main hall of the Museum für Naturkunde. The result was an immense skeleton some 75 feet (almost 23 m) long—it remains the tallest dinosaur skeleton in the world. Recently, it was dismantled and conserved for a "makeover" that included other exhibits and the museum buildings. After covering the parts in protective layers, a crane arrived to reassemble the huge skeleton. The new supports and framework allow individual bones to be removed for study. The *Brachiosaurus* "face-lift" has been literal, too, in that the front legs are straighter and the head now higher, so that the dinosaur stands almost 43 feet (13 m) tall.

Tendaguru in southeast Tanzania is a remote but rewarding destination for fossil hunters.

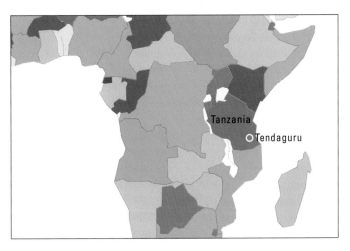

Dinosaur Desert

In 1922, one of the first major Western fossil-hunting expeditions to Asia traveled to the Gobi Desert of Mongolia—a vast region of dry scrub, rocks, and windblown dust. Organized by the American Museum of Natural

Roy Chapman Andrews in December of 1923, having returned from one of his many successful trips to Mongolia's Gobi Desert.

History in New York, the trip's original aim was to find fossils of early humans, popularly known at the time as "ape-man" or "missing links." But the Late Cretaceous geology of the region, dating back some 85–65 million years ago, precluded such discoveries. Instead, the explorers were rewarded by marvelous finds of dinosaurs and other creatures that created their own headline news.

Three world-renowned U.S. paleontologists led the expedition. Roy Chapman Andrews (1884–1960), who would in 1934 be named director of the American Museum of Natural History (AMNH), cultivated a heroic image

and ultimately had the greatest name recognition among the three men. He habitually wore a ranger hat, carried a revolver, and encouraged the image of a larger-than-life explorer. His encounters became a mainstay of "boy's own" adventure stories as he reportedly fended off bandits, poisonous snakes, and other dangers.

Henry Fairfield Osborn (1857–1935) was a biologist, comparative anatomist, and paleontologist who joined the museum in 1891 while also holding a post as professor at Columbia University. He was appointed president of the AMNH in 1908, holding that position until 1933. During his tenure, he masterminded much of the collections that make the museum world-renowned today. His paleontological career began with meeting Edward Drinker Cope in 1877. Among the dinosaur genera named by Osborn are *Ornitholestes* (1903), *Tyrannosaurus* (1905), *Pentaceratops* (1923), and *Velociraptor* (1924). One of his major paleontological interests and investigations was the evolution of elephants. However, he is also remembered as a supporter of theories of racial superiority and inferiority and of the false science of eugenics.

Walter Granger (1872–1941) was the expedition's chief paleontologist and an expert fossil-spotter. He had joined the

AMNH at the age of 17 and stayed for his whole working life. He had recognized the famous site of Bone Cabin Quarry, Wyoming, where a shepherd had built a simple shelter from the fossil dinosaur bones laying around on the ground. Granger worked in Europe and the Fayum region of Egypt and was involved in the discovery of the "Peking Man" near Beijing, China. He discovered the remains of some of the Gobi's most famous dinosaurs, including *Velociraptor*, *Oviraptor*, and *Protoceratops* (which he named in 1923), as well as extinct mammals and other vertebrates.

Harsh Conditions

Several expeditions ventured into the Gobi from 1922 to 1928. Conditions were extremely harsh. Temperatures soared to well over 100°F (45°C) by day and plunged to -20°F (-30°C) at night. The relentless wind whipped up sand-storms that covered and clogged everything with fine dust. Water, food, and other supplies were scarce. Transport was extremely difficult, with few landmarks or tracks in the vast empty landscape and with local bandits and dubious traders a constant threat.

Some of the most startling finds in Mongolia were the first-discovered dinosaur nests containing eggs. The sausage-shaped eggs were thought to have been laid by the pig-size, early horned dinosaur *Protoceratops*. In the 1990s, restudy of the material showed that the eggs actually belonged to the distinctive theropod *Oviraptor*, which had been named "egg thief" from the belief that it was stealing the eggs of *Protoceratops*; the eggs it was found with are now known to be its own eggs.

Above: Bayan Zag, or the Flaming Cliffs, is located in the harsh, arid Gobi Desert.

Below: One of the most exciting fossil deposits in the world, the name "Flaming Cliffs" was coined by Roy Chapman Andrews, who was struck by their appearance during a Mongolian sunset

The East

Above: The dragon has a long history in Chinese civilization. Dinosaur bones are still used today in traditional medicines as "dragon teeth" or "dragon bones."

Below: The team excavating at Zhoukoudian in the early 1930s included Teilhard de Chardin (far left), the famous Jesuit thinker and paleontologist, as well as Yang Zhongjian ("CC Young," third from left).

For centuries, "dragon bones" or "dragon's teeth" had been used in China for traditional ceremonies or ground into powders with supposed curative and magical powers. The first scientific studies of these fossils were carried out in China from 1915 to 1917, when Russian paleontologists recovered remains from sites in the north and took them back for study to St. Petersburg (at the time named Petrograd, then Leningrad). One of their discoveries was a large plant-eater about 25 feet (7.6 m) in length, the "duck-bill" or hadrosaur *Mandschurosaurus*, "Manchurian rep-

tile." It lived in Late Cretaceous times, and its fossils were found along the banks of the Amur River. This is probably the first officially named dinosaur from China; its restored skeleton is currently on display in St. Petersburg's museum. However, the remains are limited and the validity of the name has been questioned.

After the excitement of finding dinosaur nests and eggs in the Gobi Desert in 1923, dinosaurs were pushed into the background in the mid-1920s by the publicity surrounding "Peking Man." Named at the time as *Sinanthropus pekinensis*, this extinct human is known from the site known locally as Dragon Bone Hill, near Zhoukoudian (Chou-k'ou-tien), about 25 miles (40 km) southwest of Beijing. It has since been transferred

From the mid-1930s, Chinese paleontologists began to mount their own expeditions. One of their leaders was Yang Zhongjian (Young Chung-Chien, 1897–1979), known for convenience to many Westerners as "CC Young." Yang studied first at Beijing University, then in Munich, Germany, and returned to China to supervise many excavations at numerous sites. He remained one of China's greatest fossil experts for more than 50 years and is known as the founder of Chinese vertebrate paleontology. His work spurred the establishment of Beijing's Institute of Vertebrate Paleontology and Paleoanthropology. This houses one of the world's foremost collections of fossils, including breathtaking displays of dinosaurs and pterosaurs.

to our own genus *Homo*, as *H. erectus*. The fossils, fire hearths, burned bones, and other materials date from about 500,000 to 250,000 years ago.

Joint Expeditions

During the 1920s, several fossil-hunting expeditions were sent to China; these were organized jointly by Chinese paleontologists and those from Europe—including France and Sweden—and North America. Political events in China, however, caused increasing problems for Western paleontologists in obtaining permissions and work permits

Mandschurosaurus, one of the earliest dinosaurs officially discovered in China.

Gobi Again

The Gobi Desert of central-east Asia remained difficult for Western paleontologists to travel to throughout the mid-twentieth century because of the political situation in China and the upheavals of World War II. Many exciting fossils had been collected there during the 1920s, and European and North American expeditions wished to return.

One of the most distinctive 1920s finds was *Pinacosaurus*, "plank lizard," named by Charles Gilmore in 1923. A medium-size ankylosaur about 16 feet (5 m) long, with the typical bony club at the tail end presumably for swinging at enemies, it would become one of Asia's best known armored dinosaurs. The original specimens were from the spectacularly beautiful sandstone "Flaming Cliffs" of the Djadokhta

Protoceratops, an early ceratopsian dinosaur, was found in the Gobi Desert.

Formation, located in the Shabarakh Usu region. These Late Cretaceous rocks harbored many marvelous specimens, including *Velociraptor* and *Protoceratops*. In 1935, Yang Zhongjian came upon a specimen of *Pinacosaurus* in China's Ningxia province. In the 1970s, Teresa Maryanska found some excellent skull remains; in 1993, the remains of several juvenile *Pinacosaurus* came to light, perhaps buried and preserved—like many of the dinosaurs and other animals in this region—by a fierce, sudden Late Cretaceous sandstorm.

Polish-Mongolian Expeditions

Polish paleontologist Teresa Maryanska was a member of several joint Polish-Mongolian expeditions to the Gobi, mainly mounted during 1964–65 and 1970–71. She worked regularly with her Polish colleague Halszka Osmolska; between them they have named several important genera including the "bone-head" pachycephalosaurs *Homalocephale* and *Prenocephale* (both 1974) and the little ceratopsian *Bagaceratops* (1975), "small horn face," just 3 feet (about 1 m) in length and weighing around 50 pounds (22 kg). Indeed, Maryanska and Osmolska proposed the grouping of Pachycephalosauria in 1974.

Saichania was an ankylosaur about 20 feet (6 m) long, described and named from the Mongolian as "beautiful one" by Maryanska in 1977. The enormous arms, hands, and fingers known as *Deinocheirus* were named by Osmolska in 1970.

Tyrannosaurus is one of the most famed dinosaurs—and North American. Its Asian equivalent has been known as *Tarbosaurus*, "alarming reptile." Remains are known from the Nemegt Basin, an incredibly productive part of the Gobi for dinosaurian and other fossils. Evgeny Maleev (1915–66) described the large theropod in 1955 following its discovery during a 1948 Soviet-Mongolian expedition. In many respects, *Tarbosaurus* is similar to *Tyrannosaurus*, although generally slightly smaller and with even more diminutive arms. But it also shows similarities to the much lesser-known *Alioramus*, another Late Cretaceous theropod from Mongolia, although at an estimated 20 feet (6 m) in length, *Alioramus* was considerably smaller than *Tarbosaurus*.

Through the 1970s, further Soviet expeditions continued to find fascinating fossils of dinosaurs and other creatures in Mongolia. They include the curious *Avimimus*, "bird mimic," a small oviraptor-like theropod only about 5 feet (1.5 m) long, with a parrot-style beak. It was named by Sergei Kurzanov (who also described *Alioramus* in 1976) in 1981, from remains found in the Djadokhta Formation mentioned above.

More Chinese Finds

China had a tumultuous year in 1949, with the founding of the People's Republic. Paleontology was not a priority for the new administration. Permits for fossil hunting were often refused or granted and then inexplicably terminated. Under the leadership of Yang Zhongjian, the Institute of Vertebrate Paleontology and Paleoanthropology in Beijing became the central controlling body for fossil hunting in the nation, but its influence waned.

In 1962, Yang was joined by a young assistant who would also achieve world fame, Dong Zhiming (b. 1937). Dong had been awestruck by dinosaurs since visiting an exhibition at age 13, where he saw a fossil of a hadrosaur leg bone that was as large as he was. However, by

CHINA-CANADA DINOSAUR PROJECT

In the 1980s, Dong worked closely with Phil Currie and Dale Russell to set up the China-Canada Dinosaur Project, with the teams sharing resources and expertise. In 1994, the 25-foot (7.6 m), allosaurlike theropod *Sinraptor dongi*, "Dong's Chinese thief," was named by Currie in Dong's honor.

the mid-1960s, fossil collecting by the institute had almost ceased. Its members were commandeered for work of a more "useful" nature. Dong was sent to southwest China to carry out geological surveys for massive farmland irrigation projects. On return visits to Beijing, however, he met with Yang and discussed possible fossil finds from his surveying.

During the 1970s, Chinese collectors again visited an increasing range of sites in Yunnan, Xinjiang, Sichuan (Schezwan), and Gansu. At a quarry near Dashanpu, Sichuan, in 1979 Dong found a magnificent "dinosaur graveyard" with thousands of fossils, many of previously unknown kinds. The remains were especially valuable because they dated to the Middle Jurassic Period, about 170 million years ago, a time that is underrepresented in sites around the world.

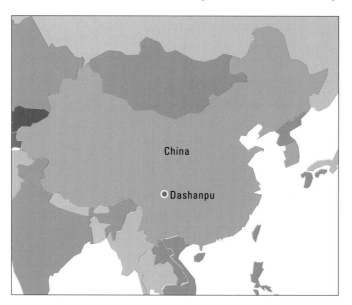

China

Dashanpu

Drowned in a Flood

The area at Dashanpu was once a lake with a river flowing into it. During floods, the bodies of dinosaurs and other creatures were carried in by the river and then rotted on the lakeshore. During the next rains the flood returned, bringing more mud and more bodies, and so on. Dong's team recovered fossils representing more than 100 dinosaurs, including the long-necked plant-eater *Shunosaurus*. In 1987, a dinosaur museum and exhibition center opened at the Dashanpu site. The amazing displays show about 15,000 sq. feet (1,300 sq. m) of bone beds—large expanses of jumbled fossilized bones lying in the rocks, not only those of dinosaurs but also those of crocodiles, fish, and pterosaurs.

Other remarkable dinosaurs were found in China during this time. *Shantungosaurus* was one of the bigger hadrosaurs (duckbills); it was named in 1973 for its discovery site in Shantung (Shandong), near Shaanxi. *Tuojiangosaurus* was a well-known stegosaur that was described in 1977 by Dong Zhiming and colleagues.

Overall, Dong is credited—usually with colleagues such as Dale Russell, Li Jinling, Tang Zilu, Zhang Zicheng, and Zhou

Shiwu—with naming more than 20 genera of dinosaurs, including the therizinosaur *Alxasaurus* (1993), the midsized theropod *Gasosaurus* (1985), the possible ornithopod *Gongbusaurus* (1983), the primitive stegosaur *Huayangosaurus* (1982), and the tiny, feathered *Sinornithoides* (1994), a cousin of *Troodon*.

Above: Visitors admire the displays at Zigong Dinosaur Museum in Zigong, Sichuan.

Below: *Shantungosaurus* is notable for its enormous size. Some paleontologists have suggested that hadrosaurs used their tails in self-defense.

CHAPTER 14

MORE AND MORE EXTREME

SINCE THE DINOSAURS WERE RECOGNIZED as a distinct group of reptiles, every decade has seen new fossil finds. In the 1960s, John Ostrom's *Deinonychus* studies encouraged theories of warm-blooded dinosaurs. In the 1970s, John "Jack" Horner and Robert Makela showed that *Maiasaura* could show parental care. Public perceptions of dinosaurs began to change. No longer slow, solitary, stupid, lumbering beasts, some dinosaurs were active, sophisticated animals with complex behaviors and social lives.

In the 1980s, marvelous new finds from South America included some of the earliest dinosaurs and large meat-eaters. In the 1990s came the discovery of the massive carnivore *Giganotosaurus* and the equally massive herbivore *Argentinosaurus*. From the 1980s through to the 2000s, the spotlight was also brightening on Madagascar, where fossil clues to some of the earliest dinosaurs were unearthed, and China, where astonishing revelations included feathered dinosaurs and Mesozoic birds. Evidence mounted that certain dinosaurs evolved into birds. Today, scientists have concluded that dinosaurs with feathers still survive today, as modern birds.

An artist's depiction of a Triassic landscape. The astonishing breadth of knowledge scientists continue to gain about long-vanished ecosystems and life-forms allows them to recreate the past in ever more accurate and varied detail.

Discoveries in the South

In 1985, eminent Argentinean paleontologist José Bonaparte (b. 1928) and colleague Fernando Novas, of the Museo Argentino de Ciencias Naturales (Argentine Museum of Natural Sciences), announced an exciting new discovery. *Abelisaurus*, "Abel's lizard," was a large theropod, perhaps exceeding 25 feet (7.6 m) in length. Named after Robert Abel—former director of the Museo de Cipolletti, in north Patagonia, who first discovered the specimen—it was excavated from the Anacleto Formation of the Comahue region, Patagonia, and is dated to the mid–Late Cretaceous, around 85–80 million years ago. *Abelisaurus* is usually included in the Ceratosauria, which includes *Ceratosaurus* itself and also

South America used to be home to some of the world's largest land animals ever to have lived, including *Argentinosaurus* and *Giganotosaurus*.

the distinctive *Carnotaurus*, described on earlier pages, which was delineated and named by Bonaparte. *Abelisaurus* is known from only one partial skull, but this was enough to compare it with *Carnotaurus*. *Abelisaurus* lacks the eyebrow "horns," and has a longer skull and jaws, in contrast to the more flattened snout of *Carnotaurus*.

Bonaparte began collecting fossils as a boy and later organized a museum in his local town. He was eventually appointed curator at the Universidad Nacional de Tucuman, in San Miguel de Tucuman, northwest Argentina, and in the late 1970s he joined the Museo Argentino de Ciencias Naturales. In 1969, he described the prosauropod *Riojasaurus*; in 1970 the bristle-toothed "broom-mouth" pterosaur *Pterodaustro*; for many years, he continued making prolific discoveries and publishing widely. Among the many dinosaurs named by Bonaparte and his colleagues are the great sauropods *Argentinosaurus* (with Coria, 1993), *Amargasaurus* (with Salgado, 1991), and the eggs and hatchlings of *Mussaurus* (1979).

Argentine Marvels

José Bonaparte has seen the rise to prominence of South America, especially Argentina, as a region for significant fossil discoveries. His work helped to show how dinosaur groups such as titanosaurs diversified and spread during the Late Cretaceous Period, when South America was isolated for long periods from other land masses.

Among Bonaparte's eminent Argentinean colleagues are Rodolfo Coria, Fernando Novas, and Leonardo Salgado. Coria, as director of the Museo Carmen Funes at Plaza Huincul, in Argentina's Neuquén Province, is noted for organizing the excavation of, describing, and naming the record-breaking carnivore *Giganotosaurus* (1995), with Salgado, and the herbivore *Argentinosaurus*, as mentioned above.

In addition to conaming *Abelisaurus*, Fernando Novas, from the Museo Argentino de Ciencias Naturales, described and named *Megaraptor* (1998) and the exceptionally birdlike *Unenlagia* (with Pablo Puerta, 1997). The single claw of Late Cretaceous *Megaraptor*, about 1 foot (30 cm) long, was thought to be from the second toe of a dromaeosaur, similar to *Velociraptor* or *Deinonychus*, but far bigger. However,

discovery of further remains of the arm indicate that the claw came from the first finger of a larger theropod, perhaps a type of allosaur.

Leonardo Salgado, of the Museo de Geología y Paleontología (Museum of Geology and Paleontology), Universidad Nacional del Comahue, Buenos Aires, recently joined a paleontology expedition with Brazilian colleagues to the Amazon region. Here they discovered the sauropod *Amazonsaurus* (2003), the first named dinosaur from that region. In 2006, Novas, Salgado, Jorge Calvo, and Federico Agnolín described the massive vertebrae and other fossils from a giant titanosaur, *Puertasaurus*, as described in chapter two.

World Renown

A global figure in the search for fossils of dinosaurs and other creatures, Paul Sereno (b. 1957) tells how a behind-the-scenes tour at the American Museum of Natural History in New York City sparked his enthusiasm for fossils and the world of exploration, science, and art. In 1987, Sereno joined the University of Chicago, and now teaches paleontology, evolution, and anatomy. The recipient of many awards and citations, he was appointed one of National Geographic's Explorers in Residence in 2000. To many, he is one of the world's most public faces for dinosaurs and paleontology.

Sereno made his first trip as expedition leader in 1988 to the mid-Late Triassic rocks of the Ischigualasto

Right: One of the more recent fossil finds, in Argentina in 1991, revealed one of the oldest dinosaurs: *Eoraptor* roamed the Late Triassic Period, and is one of the most primitive of known theropods.

Below: Paul Sereno's travels have taken him and his teams all over the world, to sites from South America to Asia.

Formation in Argentina. Fossils had been turning up in these rocky badlands for many years. As described in chapter five, one set of remains had been named *Herrerasaurus* in 1963. Sereno spotted a much more complete *Herrerasaurus* skeleton protruding from eroding sandstone. This fossil allowed detailed study and thereby generated much discussion about the status of *Herrerasaurus*. The next major expedition to the same region began in 1991—it uncovered the much smaller skeleton of an early saurischian dino-

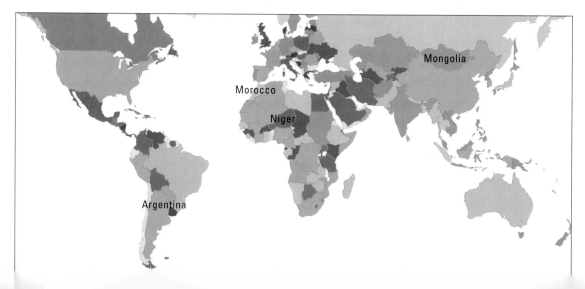

saur, *Eoraptor*, which was described and named by Sereno and colleagues Cathy Forster, Raymond Rogers, and Alfredo Monetta in 1993.

To Africa

Between 1990 and 2003, Sereno organized and led six major expeditions to Africa, most to Niger's Sahara Desert. The first journey—to the Agadez region—proved useful for learning about working in such remote, arduous terrain. Among the Early Cretaceous deposits was a "graveyard" of sauropod fossils. In 1993, the team returned and discovered the relatively complete skeleton of a large theropod. In 1994, Sereno and team members named this dinosaur *Afrovenator*, "African hunter." *Afrovenator* was about 30 feet (9 m) in length.

The 1995 expedition to Morocco yielded another huge predator, the long and slim *Deltadromeus*, and a 5-foot (1.5 m) skull of *Carcharodontosaurus*, a massive allosaurid described earlier. Back in Agadez, Niger, in 1997, the team turned up the sauropod *Jobaria* and the spinosaurid theropod *Suchomimus*, both described and named in 1998. A composite *Jobaria* skeleton suggested a total length exceeding 60 feet (18 m). *Suchomimus*, "crocodile mimic," was perhaps 40 feet (12 m) when fully

grown; its narrow, crocodilelike skull places it in the spinosaur group. In addition to dinosaurs, Sereno gained publicity from finding further and more complete remains of a huge crocodilelike reptile, *Sarcosuchus*, which had been named in 1966.

In 2001, Sereno embarked on the Chinese-American Dinosaur Expedition to the Gobi Desert of Inner Mongolia; he also visited India. He continues to travel widely and, as cofounder of the Chicago-based Project Exploration, supports personal experiences with scientists as a way to make science accessible to the public, especially younger people.

Above: The alarmingly sized jaws of *Sarcosuchus*, a crocodile of the Early Cretaceous Period, likely snapped down primarily on fish, but at nearly 6 feet (1.8 m) long, would have been big enough for nearly anything it came across.

Below: *Afrovenator*, the "African hunter," is most commonly grouped with the megalosaurs, but some have argued that it is a primitive spinosaur or even a sister genus to *Allosaurus*.

Chinese Riches

Since the mid-1990s, with the announcement of the early bird *Confuciusornis* and the feathered nonavian dinosaur *Sinosauropteryx*, paleontological and dinosaur attention has focused on the remote hills of China's rural northeastern province of Liaoning. The geology of the Yixian Formation deposits in the region show that in the Early Cretaceous Period, more than 120 million years ago, the area was a patchwork of scrub, woods, and forests interspersed with streams, rivers, and lakes—and volcanoes. Sporadic eruptions caused fine ash to rain down on the landscape. Aquatic crea-

The tropical climate of Mesozoic Mongolia was filled with feathered dinosaurs and early birds, taking to the sky for the first time.

tures, and those that died and ended up in the water, were rapidly buried in the fine-grained bottom sediments. Such fast entombment meant that little oxygen remained with the bodies, thus they decayed only slightly. Fossils were preserved in astonishing detail, often in the creature's original position, with soft tissues, even eyes and digestive organs, extant.

Apart from dinosaurs, both nonavian and avian, the formation has yielded remains of other reptiles, mammals, fish, aquatic invertebrates such as shrimps, bivalve shellfish, and aquatic snails, and also flowers and trees. The paleoecology of the region

is being reconstructed in ever-increasing detail with each exciting new find.

Everlasting Sleep

In 2004, a small, troodontidlike, nonavian dinosaur from Liaoning was described and named by Xu Xing and Mark Norrell as *Mei long*, "soundly sleeping dragon." This name was based on the posture of the preserved creature, which has its head tucked under the left forelimb, in the manner of birds—which often tuck their heads under the wing to rest and sleep (this stance helps to conserve body heat). In *Mei*, the tail also encircles the body—a mammalian behavioral trait for retaining body warmth. The troodontid group includes extremely birdlike dinosaurs, and *Mei* very well might have been sleeping when overcome by some sort of catastrophe, such as being gassed by volcanic fumes or covered by a sudden fall of volcanic ash.

A similar head-tuck posture was also seen in a less complete find of another troodontid theropod, *Sinornithoides*, in 1994. *Mei* is notable for two other reasons: It is very small, only 21 inches (53 cm) in total length; also, its three-letter genus name is the shortest of any Mesozoic dinosaur.

Other stimulating fossil finds from the Liaoning region include

the feathered early dromaeosaur *Sinornithosaurus* (found and named in 1999), the troodontid *Sinovenator* (2002), the early ceratopsian *Liaoceratops* (2002), the tiny bird *Liaoxiornis* (1999), and the bulky, cat-sized mammal *Repenomamus robustus* (2000), which has the remains of a small dinosaur, a young *Psittacosaurus*, preserved in its stomach region.

Above: The impressions of feathers prove not only that *Sinornithosaurus* was feathered, but suggests that related dinosaurs, like *Velociraptor*, were as well.

Below: This specimen of *Confuciusornis*, an early bird named after the renowned Chinese philosopher, shows what must have been a long tail.

Dinosaurs for Sale

Sue the dinosaur, one of the most complete *Tyrannosaurus rex* specimens ever found, also set a record for costliest fossil at a sale price of $8.36 million.

Fossils, especially those of dinosaurs, are big business. A quick walk around a fossil store or some internet searching reveals endless opportunities to dig up, sell, and buy the preserved remains of dinosaurs and all kinds of life-forms. One of the most famous fossil transactions was the *Tyrannosaurus* "Sue," which in 1997 cost the successful bidder, Chicago's Field Museum, a cool $8.36 million.

Like any business, commercial paleontology has its shady side, featuring get-rich-quick tricksters from outside the science, who know little about fossils but plenty about how to turn a fast buck. However, the scientific establishment is occasionally involved. In the mid-nineteenth century, Richard Owen tried to take credit for Gideon Mantell's discoveries. During the "Bone Wars" of Marsh and Cope, fossils of rival teams were faked, planted, copied, and smashed. In 1912, "Piltdown Man," the "apeman" many scientists expected to find, made headlines, but in 1953 it was exposed as a hoax.

Composite Specimen

A cautionary tale began in 1998 with the unveiling of what seemed to be a classic dinosaur-bird "missing link." It was a fossil slab showing nonavian dinosaur and bird features from the Early Cretaceous deposits of Liaoning, in northeast China. Dubbed "Archaeoraptor," it was purchased for $80,000 by a private museum. In 1999, an article in *National Geographic* bestowed the provisional name "Archaeoraptor" and emphasized the fossil's value.

However, parallel investigations were checking the fossil's validity. Very close study of the specimen by experienced paleontologists, including Phil Currie, Tim Rowe (who carried out the CT scan), and

Xu Xing, showed that it was a fake. Broadly, it had been made by gluing together the preserved head and body of a bird, with the tail and parts of the back legs of a nonavian dinosaur. Currie, one of Canada's greatest paleontologists, has worked extensively on the links between nonavian and avian dinosaurs, and on patterns of evolution and extinction.

A Liaoning farmer probably carried out the initial "Archaeoraptor" hoax. The specimen should not have been available in the United States, however, because China banned exports of fossils. Further studies surprisingly revealed that both the bird and the nonavian dinosaur were seemingly new to science. In April 2000, the avian part of the hoax specimen was initially renamed *Archaeovolans repatriatus*. The species was, in actuality, already known as *Yanornis*, thus that name took priority. *Yanornis* was a pigeon-sized flier with teeth in its jaws that also possessed characteristics similar to more modern birds.

In a further twist, Xu Xing and colleagues who investigated the fraud managed to locate the counterpart ("mirror image") of the tail—plus the rest of the creature. They described and named it in late 2000 as the tiny feathered dromaeosaur *Microraptor zhaoianus* (*Microraptor gui* is covered in chapter four). But the tail part of the original "Archaeoraptor" had already been named more firmly in a newsletter article. Discussions about which of these names should take priority were colored by the tainted associations of "Archaeoraptor." The species is now generally known as *Microraptor zhaoianus*.

Changing Times

Right: The modern paleontology lab is kept clean and organized. Bones are carefully catalogued and examined with a plethora of scientific and forensic equipment.

Below: At Dinosaur National Monument, a paleontologist carefully chips away at surrounding rock to reveal a dinosaur's backbone.

In some respects the search for, excavation of, and study of fossils have changed enormously—not only in the past 200 years but even in the past 20. What would Marsh, Cope, Brown, Nopcsa, Hennig, Janensch, and Granger make of a modern fossil expedition? Doubtless they would sympathize with the extreme conditions of heat, cold, wind, humidity, glaring sun, and problems with water, food, and other resources. They might recognize many of the tools and techniques, but raise eyebrows at modern equipment and technology such as satellite imaging, laptop computers, GPS (global positioning system) receivers, and at how the mass of data is now sifted and analyzed using computer programs. They might also appreciate medical progress in areas such as antibiotics and other drugs

for treating infections and illness, and advice on limiting sun exposure to avoid skin cancers.

Great changes have also occurred in the public perception of Mesozoic dinosaurs. One of the first to challenge their reputation as slow, cold, and stupid was John Ostrom (1928–2005), with his landmark studies of *Deinonychus* in the 1960s. He opened the way for consideration of nonavian dinosaurs as quick, agile, and warm-blooded—or, at least, as having some metabolic control over their body temperature. Ostrom's student Robert Bakker (b. 1945) continued to pursue these ideas into the realms of paleo-ecology and speculations on dinosaur behavior, especially with his aptly titled book, *The Dinosaur Heresies* (1986).

Extending Range

Mesozoic dinosaur fossils have been found on every continent, including Antarctica. Former curator at Queensland Museum, Australia, Ralph Molnar has described several Australian representatives, including the small, widespread ankylosaur *Minmi* (1980), and the large ornithopod *Muttaburrasaurus* (1981). Thomas Rich and Patricia Vickers-Rich are well known for their studies of the much smaller Australian ornithopod *Leaellynasaura* found at the ocean cliff site of Dinosaur Cove.

European Finds

Several notable discoveries have been made in Europe. Near Riodeva, about 25 miles (40 km) from Teruel, in east-central Spain, local people cleared almond orchards of troublesome stones for centuries. In 2003, paleontologists Rafael Royo and Alberto Cobos discovered that the "stones" were fossil fragments. One of

their finds was a large sauropod—the biggest dinosaur known so far from Europe. *Turiasaurus riodevensis* was named in 2006 for the Turia (Teruel) region and Riodeva village. It weighed an estimated 40-plus tons and perhaps exceeded 100 feet (30 m) in length.

The Isle of Wight, off the southern coast of England, is famed for its Cretaceous fossils. In 1978, parts of a large theropod were spotted protruding from the eroding chalk cliffs. Further excavations carried out in the 1990s resulted in *Neovenator*, "new hunter," a large predator about 25 feet (7.6 m) long, slim in build, and probably a relative of *Allosaurus*. It lived in the Early Cretaceous Period, about 120 million years ago.

To accurately map fossil discoveries, paleontologists first divide the site into numbered squares.

Today and Tomorrow

Phil Currie and his team work at Red Deer River in Alberta, Canada. Much has been accomplished since the first dinosaur was named in 1824, but there is still much more from the ancient world of dinosaurs to find.

As the twenty-first century unfolds, China continues to provide spectacular fossils. Xu Xing, researcher at the Institute of Vertebrate Paleontology and Paleoanthropology, was instrumental in sorting out the "Archaeoraptor"/ *Microraptor* affair described earlier. He has studied and named, with coworkers, numerous genera—several included in this book—including the curious therizinosaur *Beipiaosaurus*, the early ceratopsian *Yinlong*, and the head-tucked-under-arm troodontid *Mei*. In 2006, Xu and colleagues described what could be a very early form of tyrannosaur, *Guanlong*. It was only about 10 feet (3 m) long and lived during the Late Jurassic, some 160 million years ago. Its fossils come from China's Dzungaria region, in the northwest of the country.

Across the Pacific Ocean in California, Argentinian-born Luis M. Chiappe works as associate curator and chairman of the Department of Vertebrate Paleontology, Natural History Museum of Los Angeles County. Chiappe has searched for fossils of dinosaurs, pterosaurs, crocodiles, and other vertebrates, especially in Patagonia, Argentina, and the Gobi Desert in Mongolia. His 2001 book with Lowell Dingus, *Walking on Eggs*, detailed the momentous discovery of thousands of fossilized sauropod eggs in Patagonia.

Dinosaurs in the Modern World

Those within the fields of dinosaurian paleontology, paleobiology, and paleoecology are busy advancing knowledge of the great beasts and their times. In 2001, Kristi Curry Rogers, assistant curator of paleontology at the Science Museum of Minnesota, conamed the exceptionally complete juvenile *Rapetosaurus*, a Late Cretaceous titanosaur from Madagascar. She has a special interest in the titanosaurs, their spread and evolution; she is also involved in research on bone tissue, how it fossilizes, and what it tells us about the animal's growth, metabolism, and lifestyle. Curry Rogers has worked in many countries, including Madagascar, which is one of the "dinosaur hot spots" of this century, and Zimbabwe. One of many recent finds from Madagascar is the Late Cretaceous *Masiakasaurus*, "vicious (from the Malagasy *masiaka*) lizard," a curious smallish theropod with forward-pointing teeth.

Jeffrey Wilson, professor and associate curator at the Museum of Paleontology, University of Michigan, is a specialist in cladistic techniques and in untangling evolutionary relationships, especially among titanosaurs. He was able to show that the Gobi sauropod *Nemegtosaurus* was probably a titanosaur rather than a diplodocid. With Paul Sereno and Suresh Srivastava, Wilson described the Indian theropod *Rajasaurus*, "princely lizard," a 30-foot (9 m) meat-eater of the ceratosaur-abelisaur type.

Oliver Rauhut, from Munich's Bayerische Staatssammlung fuer Palaeontologie und Geologie (Bavarian State Collection for Paleontology and Geology), investigates biodiversity and biogeography as manifested by meat-eating dinosaurs from the southern continents; he also examines how the various groups diversified there.

Matthew Carrano, curator of dinosaurs at the National Museum of Natural History, Smithsonian Institution, Washington, D.C., investigates the evolutionary relationships between dinosaur groups and other vertebrates, with the goal of identifying large-scale patterns of evolution, clarifying understanding of Gondwanan dinosaur evolution, and filling in gaps in the evolutionary record. He has worked in Africa, Madagascar, and Chile, as well as nearer home in Wyoming.

A Global Pursuit

New generations of paleontologists continue to build on the work of earlier experts. The scientific framework of cladistic phylogenetics provides exciting and fruitful methods of assessing and comparing finds, making proposals, and testing them against available evidence. New techniques in many scientific fields, from radiometric dating and microscopy to genetic materials analysis, provide ever-increasing amounts of data for computer-aided analysis. Worldwide communications improve year by year, allowing experts to share their information and debate views. Never has dinosaurian paleontology been such an active, progressive, and global pursuit.

Glossary

AGE OF DINOSAURS. Colloquial term for the Mesozoic Era, 251–65 million years ago; time period in which nonavian dinosaurs were the dominant life forms.

AMNIOTIC EGG. A hard-shelled egg in which internal membranes hold in moisture for the developing embryo, allowing the egg to be laid on land. A defining feature of amniotes.

ANGIOSPERM. Flowering plants; first appeared in the Cretaceous.

ARCHOSAUR. A grouping of diapsid amniotes that first developed in the Late Permian; includes all dinosaurs as well as modern crocodiles and alligators, as well as birds.

ASTEROID. A small rocky body in orbit around the Sun, distinguished from planets primarily by size.

ASTRAGALUS. An ankle bone whose arrangement is one of several features that may be used to identify dinosaurs.

BASAL. An early or primitive bodily feature, structure, or organism.

BIOMECHANICS. The study of the mechanics of biological systems and structures.

BIPEDAL. Propelled on the ground by two limbs, such as birds and other theropod dinosaurs.

BIRD. Member of the class Aves. By current phylogenic understanding, the only remaining members of the dinosaur clade.

CARBONIFEROUS PERIOD. The Period spanning 360–299 million years ago. Preceded by the Devonian and fol-lowed by the Permian, the Carboniferous Period is so named for the coal beds found in Western Europe that date to this time. Scientists believe that amniotes may have developed in this time.

CARNIVORE. An organism whose diet consists primarily of meat.

CENOZOIC. Literally, "recent life;" the present Era, which began 65.5 million years ago.

CLADE. A genetic grouping consisting of the most recent common ancestor of a set of organisms and all of its descendants.

COPROLITE. Fossilized scat, or dung. Coprolites can reveal the diet of extinct animals.

CRETACEOUS. The Period spanning 145–65 million years ago; the third and final portion of the Mesozoic Era.

DIAPSID. A reptile with two temporal fenestrae on either side of the skull; includes all dinosaurs, lizards, crocodiles, and snakes.

DIG SITE. An apportioned area where paleontologists are currently looking for fossils.

DINOSAUR. A member of the taxon Dinosauria, distinguished from other archosaurs by a suite of skeletal features, including a specialized neck, long arms, and a hole in the acetabulum.

ECOSYSTEM. An interrelated set of environmental conditions and living organisms that is self-sustaining in a natural form.

ECTOTHERMY. The ability to control internal body temperature by absorbing external heat. Crocodiles and lizards are ectotherms.

ENDOCRANIAL CAST. A cast made of the brain cavity of a fossilized skull. Scientists study endocranial casts to make inferences about intelligence and other aspects of long-dead creatures.

ENDOTHERMY. The ability to control internal body temperature by generating heat from internal processes such as food digestion and muscle contraction. Mammals and birds are endotherms.

EVOLUTION. Change through time. Species evolve from other species by accumulating changes over many generations, so that they become distinct, reproductively isolated organisms.

EVOLUTIONARY RADIATION. A relatively sudden increase in the number of species within a set of organisms. For instance, from being exclusively small and rodentlike, mammals radiated in the geologically short space of 30 million years or so into many of the forms known today.

EXCAVATION. Process of discovery in the fields of paleontology and archeology; here, the uncovering of fossilized remains or trace evidence of dead organisms.

FAMILY. A taxonomic unit of classification ranking below order and containing one or more related genera.

FENESTRAE (singular: fenestra). Literally, windows; gaps in bone structures. Placement and number can be used as taxonomic distinguishing features.

FOSSIL. Preserved remains or traces of any evidence of past life.

FOSSIL RECORD. All of the fossils ever discovered and recorded by science.

GASTROLITH. A stone that has been deliberately swallowed to aid in digestion. Ostrichs demonstrate this behavior, and it is believed that oviraptorosaurs, ornithomimosaurs, and possibly some sauropods did as well.

GENUS. A taxonomic unit that includes one or more related species. For example, *Homo sapiens* includes the taxonomic genus name, *Homo*, and species name, *sapiens*, for human beings.

GIGANTOTHERMY. Phenomenon by which an organism maintains a high level of thermal inertia (constant body temperature) by being large (having a high ratio of body mass to skin area).

GONDWANA. The southern half of Pangaea; a separate continent comprising modern South America, Africa, India, Australia, and Madagascar.

GREENHOUSE EFFECT. A phenomenon in which the average temperature of Earth rises due to gases or debris trapping the Sun's heat.

HABITAT. One or more ecosystems forming a distinct region where one or more organisms naturally live.

HELL CREEK FORMATION. A Late Cretaceous rock formation in the north-northwestern United States. Significant dinosaur and other fossil finds have been discovered here.

HERBIVORE. An organism whose diet consists primarily of plant material.

ICE AGE. A period of reduced global temperature during which glaciers often cover much of the Earth's surface.

ICHTHYOSAUR. A large, aquatic reptile, in appearance like a modern shark or porpoise; largely contemporary with the nonavian dinosaurs.

INVERTEBRATE. An organism without bones; the vast majority of animal species.

ISCHIGUALASTO FORMATION. A geologic layer in northwest Argentina containing fossils from the Late Triassic Period, some of which, like *Eoraptor* and *Herrerasaurus*, are the oldest dinosaurs ever found. The Ischigualasto Formation is found in the Valley of the Moon, so-called for its bizarre-looking eroded rock structures in a dry, vast expanse.

JURASSIC. The Period spanning 200–145 million years ago; the middle portion of the Mesozoic Era.

K/T BOUNDARY. The abrupt change in rock types identified as the boundary between the Cretaceous Period (K) and the Paleogene (Pg) or the older geologic terminology of Tertiary (T).

K/T MASS EXTINCTION. The mass extinction event at the end of the Cretaceous. Although many details are still unknown, many believe that an asteroid striking the Earth caused most life on the planet to be wiped out, including all nonavian dinosaurs.

LAURASIA. The northern half of Pangaea; a separate continent comprised of modern North America, Asia, Greenland, and Europe.

LIMESTONE. A form of rock that may preserve particularly detailed fossils, most

notably traces of ancient feathers and similarly delicate structures.

LITHOGRAPHIC. A type of limestone found in Solnhofen, Germany. It received its name from its early use in printing; paleontologists appreciate it for its detailed fossils of specimens like *Archaeopteryx*.

MAASTRICHTIAN. The final stage of the Cretaceous Period. Lasting from 70.6–65.5 million years ago, the Maastrichtian ended in the mass extinction event that wiped out most of Earth's living organisms in the K/T mass extinction.

MASS EXTINCTION. An extinction event in which the majority of species living at the time of the event is wiped out. While rare, such events have occurred with varying intensity at multiple times in the history of life on earth.

MESOZOIC. The Era spanning 251–65 million years ago. Covers the Triassic, Jurassic, and Cretaceous Periods and is colloquially known as the "Age of Dinosaurs." Preceded by the Paleozoic, "first life," and followed by the Cenozoic, "new life," Mesozoic literally means "middle life," referring to its intermediary position in the history of life on Earth.

METEORITE. A rocky body that has impacted with Earth.

MISSING LINK. A popular but somewhat inaccurate term to describe an organism in an apparently transitional stage between two known members of an evolutionary branch.

NATURAL SELECTION. The mechanism by which evolution occurs. Small differences between individuals allow some to succeed better than others when faced with environmental pressures. The surviving organisms produce more off-spring, allowing their unique features to become more common in the population. Thus the natural world "selects" advantageous features over time, eventually leading to the evolution of a new species from its ancestor.

NEOGENE. The Period beginning 23 million years ago and continuing today.

OLIGOCENE. The Epoch spanning 34–24 million years ago; toward the middle of the Cenozoic Era.

OMNIVORE. An organism whose diet consists of both plant and animal materials. Human beings and most bears are modern examples of omnivorous creatures.

ORNITHISCHIA. One of the two major groups in the dinosaur clade (also see Saurischia). Ornithischian, or "bird-hipped" dinosaurs are identified by their hip arrangement, in which the pubis is parallel with and lies directly against the ischium, as in modern birds. Despite this similarity, modern birds actually evolved from saurischian dinosaurs.

ORNITHOPOD. Literally, "bird-foot;" a group of ornithischian dinosaurs characterized by a three-toed foot (although some early forms retained four). One of the last and largest types of ornithopods were the hadrosaurs.

PALEOBIOLOGY. The study of the history of biological systems; combines the fields of biology and paleontology.

PALEOECOLOGY. The study of ancient ecosystems.

PALEOGENE. The Period spanning

65.5–23 million years ago; the initial Period of the Cenozoic Era.

PALEONTOLOGY. The study of the fossil record and associated once-living organisms.

PALEOZOIC. The Era spanning 542–251 million years ago; literally "first life," the earliest Era in the history of visible life on earth.

PANGAEA. The massive supercontinent of the early Mesozoic Era; it began to break up into modern continents by the end of the Triassic.

PELVIS. The hip bones. Their arrangement not only is a primary feature in identifying dinosaurs but in distinguishing between major types of dinosaurs.

PERMIAN. The Period spanning 300–251 million years ago; the final Period of the Paleozoic Era.

PHYLOGENETIC INFERENCE. Process by which scientists construct genetic relationships among organisms by filling in missing data with known relationships.

PHYSIOLOGY. The interrelated set of systems of an organism, including physical, biomechanical, and biochemical processes.

PISCIVORE. An organism whose diet consists primarily of fish.

PLATE TECTONICS. Theory that explains the drift of Earth's continents by examining the underlying plates and how they move and interact.

PLIOCENE. The Epoch roughly between 5 and 2 million years ago; the last epoch of what was once called the Tertiary Period.

POPULATION. A group of organisms inhabiting the same area and therefore more likely to reproduce within the group than with other species members.

PTEROSAUR. A member of the order Pterosauria, "winged lizard." Although frequently referred to as dinosaurs, this classification is incorrect. The first vertebrates to achieve flight, pterosaurs existed from the Late Triassic to the end of the Cretaceous, roughly the same period as nonavian dinosaurs.

REPTILE. Member of the class Reptilia. Contains subclasses of anapsids, such as turtles, and diapsids, such as dinosaurs and birds. More traditionally, includes all amniotes except for mammals.

SANDSTONE. A type of rock composed primarily of quartz and feldspar minerals.

SANTA MARÍA FORMATION. A geological layer in southern Brazil notable for its Triassic fossils. Among these are some of the earliest known dinosaur forms.

SAURISCHIA. One of two major groups in the dinosaur clade (also see Ornithischia). Saurischian, or "lizard-hipped," dinosaurs are identified by their hip arrangement in which the pubis points forward as in modern lizards. By current phylogenic understanding, birds are saurischian dinosaurs.

SAUROPOD. Literally, "lizard-feet;" large, herbivorous, quadrupedal members of order Saurischia. Along with theropods, one of two major groupings of saurischian dinosaurs.

SEXUAL DIMORPHISM. Phenomenon in which one gender of a species appears different from the other due to differentiation in size, coloration, absence versus presence of horns, crests, etc., or other such features. For example, in most mammalian species, males are larger than females.

SPECIES. A unit of biological classification, often defined as a set of organisms capable of naturally reproducing viable and fertile offspring.

SPECIMEN. Any fossilized remains, complete or not, of an organism.

SUPERNOVA. The explosive event when a massive star (a star must be at least eight times larger than the Sun to cause a supernova) runs out of hydrogen and explodes. Some scientists have proposed that a supernova caused or helped to cause the K/T mass extinction.

TERTIARY. Previously, the Period including the Paleocene through Pliocene Epochs; an interval of time spanning 65.5–1.6 million years ago. Now a discontinued term, except its abbreviation is still commonly used in discussions of the mass extinction at the end of the Cretaceous Period.

TETHYS SEA. Ancient ocean of the Cenozoic Era, stretching between the areas of modern India, Indonesia, and parts of southern Europe. Of particular importance for paleontologists for its long-term fossil record.

THERMAL INERTIA. A metabolic state in which body temperature remains relatively high and stable.

THERMOREGULATION. The process by which an organism maintains a certain body temperature or a temperature within an acceptable range.

ERA	PERIOD	EPOCH
Cenozoic	Neogene	Holocene
		Pleistocene
		Pliocene
		Miocene
	Paleogene	Oligocene
		Eocene
		Paleocene
Mesozoic	Cretaceous	
	Jurassic	
	Triassic	
Paleozoic	Permian	
	Carboniferous	
	Devonian	
	Silurian	
	Ordovician	
	Cambrian	

THEROPOD. Literally, "beast-feet;" mostly carnivorous, bipedal, saurischian dinosaurs. Along with sauropods, one of the two major groups in the Saurischia order.

TRIASSIC. The Period spanning 251–200 million years ago; the first portion of the Mesozoic Era.

TRILOBITE. A type of arthropod (the largest group of animals, which includes insects, arachnids, and others) whose excellent fossil record spans almost all of the Paleozoic Era.

VERTEBRA. One of many bones between the head and the end of the tail, if present; individual pieces of the spine or backbone. One of the early developments of a major branch of life and the distinguishing feature of vertebrate animals. Cervical vertebrae are vertebrae in the neck; dorsal are those in the back; caudal are those of the tail; and sacral are those at the hips.

VERTEBRATE. An organism with vertebrae; includes only a tiny minority of animal species.

VESTIGE. The remnant of a once-functional body part that has shrunk or become nonfunctional due to evolutionary change.

Find Out More

BOOKS

Bakker, Robert T. *The Dinosaur Heresies: New Theories Unlocking the Mystery of the Dinosaurs and Their Extinction*. Citadel, 2001.

Barrett, Paul, Raul Martin (Illustrator), and Kevin Padian (Introduction). *National Geographic Dinosaurs*. National Geographic Children's Books, 2001.

Bishop, Nic. *Digging for Bird Dinosaurs: An Expedition to Madagascar. (Scientists in the Field Series)*. Houghton Mifflin, 2002.

Carpenter, Kenneth. *The Armored Dinosaurs. (Life of the Past)*. Indiana University Press, 2001.

———. *The Carnivorous Dinosaurs. (Life of the Past)*. Indiana University Press, 2005.

———. *Horns And Beaks: Ceratopsian And Ornithopod Dinosaurs. (Life of the Past)*. Indiana University Press, 2007.

Carrano, Matthew T., Richard W. Blob, Timothy J. Gaudin, and John R. Wible. *Amniote Paleobiology: Perspectives on the Evolution of Mammals, Birds, and Reptiles*. University Of Chicago Press (New Edition), 2006.

Chiappe, Luis M. *Glorified Dinosaurs: The Origin and Early Evolution of Birds*. Wiley-Liss, 2007.

Currie, Philip J., Eva B. Koppelhus, Martin A. Shugar, and Joanna L. Wright. *Feathered Dragons: Studies on the Transition from Dinosaurs to Birds. (Life of the Past)*. Indiana University Press, 2004.

Curry Rogers, Kristina, and Jeffrey Wilson. *The Sauropods: Evolution and Paleobiology*. University of California Press, 2005.

Dingus, Lowell, Luis M. Chiappe, and Rodolfo A. Coria. *Dinosaur Eggs Discovered!: Unscrambling the Clues (Discovery)*. Twenty-First Century Books, 2007.

Dixon, Dougal. *Dinosaurs*. Boyds Mills Press (Revised Edition), 2007.

———. *The Illustrated Encyclopedia of Dinosaurs: The Ultimate Reference to 355 Dinosaurs from the Triassic, Jurassic and Cretaceous Eras*. Lorenz Books, 2007.

Fastovsky, David E., David B. Weishampel, and John Sibbick (Illustrator). *The Evolution and Extinction of the Dinosaurs*. Cambridge University Press, 2005.

Foster, John. *Jurassic West: The Dinosaurs of the Morrison Formation and Their World. (Life of the Past)*. Indiana University Press, 2007.

Fraser, Nicholas, James O. Farlow, ed., and Douglas Henderson (Illustrator). *Dawn of the Dinosaurs: Life in the Triassic*. Indiana University Press, 2006.

Gasparini, Zulma, Rodolfo A. Coria, and Leonardo Salgado, *Patagonian Mesozoic Reptiles. (Life of the Past)*. Indiana University Press, 2007.

Hallam, Tony. *Catastrophes and Lesser Calamities: The Causes of Mass Extinctions*. Oxford University Press, 2005.

Holtz, Thomas R., Jr., and Luis V. Rey (Illustrator). *Dinosaurs*. Random House Books for Young Readers, 2007.

Jaffe, Mark. *The Gilded Dinosaur: The Fossil War Between E. D. Cope and O. C. Marsh and the Rise of American Science*. Three Rivers Press, 2001.

Kerley, Barbara, and Brian Selznick (Illustrator). *The Dinosaurs of Waterhouse Hawkins: An Illuminating History of Mr. Waterhouse Hawkins, Artist and Lecturer*. Scholastic Press, 2001.

Lecointre, Guillaume, Hervé Le Guyader, Dominique Visset (Illustrator), and Karen McCoy (Translator). *The Tree of Life: A Phylogenetic Classification. (Harvard University Press Reference Library)*. Belknap Press, 2007.

Martin, Anthony, and Giuseppe Bertola. *Introduction to the Study of Dinosaurs*. Blackwell Publishing, 2006.

Norell, Mark A., and Mick Ellison, *Unearthing the Dragon*. Pi Press, 2005.

Nothdurft, William, and Josh Smith. *The Lost Dinosaurs of Egypt*. Random House, 2002.

Paul, Gregory, ed. *The Scientific American Book of Dinosaurs*. St. Martin's Griffin, 2003.

Rich, Thomas Hewitt, and Patricia Vickers-Rich. *Dinosaurs of Darkness. (Life of the Past)*. Indiana University Press, 2000.

———. *Polar Dinosaurs*. Museum Victoria Nature, 2007.

Richardson, Hazel. *Dinosaurs and Other Prehistoric Animals. (Smithsonian Handbooks)*. Dorling Kindersley, 2003.

Scotchmoor, Judith G., Dale A. Springer, Brent H. Breithaupt, and Anthony R. Fiorillo. *Dinosaurs: The Science Behind the Stories.* American Geological Institute, 2002.

Sheen, Martin. *Dinosaurs.* Dorling Kindersley, 2007

Tidwell, Virginia, and Kenneth Carpenter. *Thunder-lizards: The Sauropodomorph Dinosaurs. (Life of the Past).* Indiana University Press, 2005.

Ward, Peter Douglas, and David W. Ehlert (Illustrator). *Out of Thin Air: Dinosaurs, Birds, And Earth's Ancient Atmosphere.* Joseph Henry Press, 2006.

Weishampel, David B., Peter Dodson, Halszka Osmolska. *Dinosauria.* University of California Press, 2007.

WEB SITES

CHINESE DINOSAURS GALORE
http://www.austmus.gov.au/chinese_dinosaurs
Amazing recent discoveries of dinosaurs and other fossil creatures from China, hosted by the Australian Museum Online site.

DINO-WORLD FEENIXX POSTERS AND INFORMATION
http://www.dinosaur-world.com
Provided by the publishers of popular content-intensive info-posters.

LONDON'S NATURAL HISTORY MUSEUM DINO-DIRECTORY
http://internt.nhm.ac.uk/jdsml/nature-online/dino-directory/
A guide to more than 300 of the most well-described dinosaurs, including more than 1,000 images and an introduction to the features of dinosaurs.

NEW YORK'S AMERICAN MUSEUM OF NATURAL HISTORY DINOSAUR EXHIBITIONS
http://www.amnh.org/exhibitions/dino-saurs/
Displays and exhibitions on dinosaur biomechanics, trackways, extinctions, and meet the staff.

ONLINE DINOSAUR DIRECTORY LISTINGS
http://www.dinodirectory.com/
Directory of dinosaurs provides resources with categorized listings of names, facts, dinosaur museums, fossils, and dinosaurs around the world.

SMITHSONIAN'S NATIONAL MUSEUM OF NATURAL HISTORY DINOSAUR RESOURCES
http://paleobiology.si.edu/dinosaurs/index.htm
Fieldwork, expeditions, exhibitions, FAQs, collections, behind-the-scenes tours, interactive dino-digs, and much more.

WIKIPEDIA'S DINOSAUR HUB
http://en.wikipedia.org/wiki/Dinosaur
Jumping-off point for numerous, extensive, occasionally opinionated articles on dinosaur groups, genera, and species from the online encyclopedia.

ZOOM DINOSAURS FOR YOUNGER PEOPLE
http://www.enchantedlearning.com/subjects/dinosaurs
Popular Enchanted Learning hypertext site with extensive data on hundreds of dinosaurs and other fossil creatures, fact sheets, special features and more, prepared from basic to advanced levels for younger people.

At the Smithsonian

The largest museum complex in the world is a fitting place to experience and study the largest creatures ever to walk the Earth. Founded in 1846, the Smithsonian Institution now comprises 16 museums, 4 research centers, and the National Zoo, as well as libraries and other business ventures. It is one of the foremost institutions in the world for dinosaur research and contains an immense collection of fossils and specimens.

The National Museum of Natural History was opened in 1910. The museum has more than 1,500 catalogued dinosaur fossils in its collections.

The National Museum of Natural History

Occupying a 1.5 million square foot (457,200 sq m) building on the National Mall, the National Museum of Natural History (NMNH) more than fulfills James Smithson's hopes for the museum as "an establishment for the increase and diffusion of knowledge." Opened in 1910, the green-domed building was first officially called the National Museum of Natural History in 1967. The NMNH's collections have

grown so large that a separate facility in Suitland, Maryland is also required for storage of the more than 125 million cultural artifacts and scientific specimens owned by the museum. It is a collection as diverse as it is large, including roughly 30 million specimens of insects, 4.5 million preserved plants, 7 million fish, and 2 million cultural artifacts, including photographs and other scientifically significant miscellany. The NMNH loans more than 3.5 million specimens every year and is an invaluable resource for the world scientific community.

The NMNH also employs a varied staff of research professionals. Some work out of the historic building on the National Mall, but many conduct studies at a number of unique locations around the world. The NMNH maintains a marine science facility in Ft. Pierce, Florida, as well as field stations in Belize, Alaska, and Kenya.

The Paleobiology Department

Dinosaurs still walk the halls of the Paleobiology Department, and their presence has made it quite possibly the most popular branch of the NMNH. The "terrible lizards" are not the only focus of the department—its collections also contain millions of fossilized plants, animals, unicellular organisms, and geo-

logic specimens. However, it is the more than 1,500 catalogued dinosaur fossils in the museum's collection that attract the most attention from the public. Roughly

30 such specimens are generally on display, with 6 of the museum's dinosaurs being notable as the original specimens used to coin the name of their species.

Othniel Charles Marsh, the pioneering paleontologist who was famous for, among other endeavors, his "Bone Wars" with fellow paleontologist Edward D. Cope, is the source of the bulk of the Smithsonian's dinosaur collection. Marsh had conducted extensive field expeditions for the U.S. Geological Survey. Upon his death in 1899, the more than 80 tons of vertebrate fossils that Marsh had found for

One of the most intact *Allosaurus* skeletons ever mounted in a museum, the *Allosaurus* on display at the NMNH was found by Othniel Charles Marsh, the famous nineteenth-century paleontologist.

a massive *Diplodocus* skeleton, still a centerpiece of the NMNH's exhibited collection. Also, early in his career, before becoming curator, Gilmore helped prepare the first complete, fully mounted dinosaur skeletons at the Smithsonian. *Edmontosaurus* was exhibited in 1903; *Triceratops* followed in 1905. Both of these specimens can still be seen today.

Above: The Smithsonian Institution has displayed dinosaur skeletons since 1910. At one time called the "Hall of Extinct Monsters," the NMNH's Dinosaur Hall attracts millions of visitors every year.

Right: This *Allosaurus* foot, displayed at the NMNH, dates from the Late Jurassic Period, roughly 145 million years ago.

the government were turned over to the Smithsonian. This collection provided some of the Smithsonian's most recognized specimens, including fossils of *Allosaurus*, *Ceratosaurus*, *Edmontosaurus*, *Stegosaurus*, and *Triceratops*.

The Twentieth Century

Charles W. Gilmore made 16 dinosaur expeditions as the Smithsonian Curator of Fossil Reptiles, obtained many of the Smithsonian's notable dinosaur fossils, and was instrumental in establishing the Smithsonian as a center for dinosaur research and collection. During his 21-year tenure (1924–45), Gilmore emerged as one of the most famous vertebrate paleontologists of his time and named a multitude of new species. One of his more noteworthy discoveries was

In 1910, the dinosaur collections were consolidated inside the U.S. National Museum, which is now the National Museum of Natural History. The Hall of Extinct Monsters was soon opened, displaying many of the mounted dinosaurs for which the Smithsonian is still famous.

The venue has undergone many changes throughout the twentieth century—the Dinosaur Hall was renovated twice, in the early 1960s and late 1970s, and more recently, the fossils of *Triceratops* and *Stegosaurus*, weathered by nearly a century on display amid ambient humidity and the crush of visitors, have been removed for conservation and replaced with plaster casts in more accurate and dynamic poses.

A New Era

The future of the Paleobiology Department is bound to be exciting in a time of ever-expanding scholarship and enthusiasm for dinosaurs. In 2003, Matthew Carrano became the museum's first official Curator of Dinosaurs. He led recent fossil-finding expeditions to both Wyoming and Madagascar. His focus is "large-scale evolutionary patterns within the Dinosauria." By studying the evolutionary fluctuations of dinosaurs, animals that dominated habitats for millions of years, he is revealing more about the intricate processes of evolution, which inherently shape all life on Earth.

More than 20 million people visit the Smithsonian Institution annually. No doubt a great many of them are attracted by the towering fossils of Dinosaur Hall. Come see the *Allosaurus*, *Diplodocus*, *Stegosaurus*, *Triceratops*, and countless others for yourself, and while you are at it, walk across the Mall to visit the other Smithsonian museums. Man or beast, there is truly something here for everybody.

For more information about the history of dinosaur paleontology at the Smithsonian, visit http://paleobiology. si.edu/dinosaurs/ collection/history/main.html. Admission is free at all museums of the Smithsonian Institution; normal operating hours are 10 a.m. to 5:30 p.m. daily. E-mail info@si.edu or phone (202) 633-1000.

Left: The skull of this duck-billed dinosaur, on display at the NMNH, shows the multiple rows of teeth nestled in the sides of its jaws. The teeth were worn down and replaced continuously throughout the dinosaur's life.

Below: Matthew Carrano, the Smithsonian's Curator of Dinosaurs, analyzing a fossil. In studying the evolution of dinosaurs, Carrano is seeking a greater understanding of large-scale evolutionary patterns.

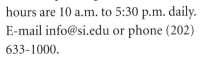

Index

Acknowledgments and Credits

Steve Parker: Some years ago while on the London Natural History Museum staff, I was inspired by the breadth of knowledge and clarity of thought of senior paleontologist Colin Patterson, in his lecturing, writing, and informal discussion. I thank him for showing how it could be done. Several fossil experts have contributed to ideas and approach, from world-renowned paleontologist Philip Currie to our trusty band of local enthusiasts such as Stephen Dean, Chris Hall, and Peter Coates. Dr. Jason Head has been truly invaluable as text commentator for this book, and I appreciate his wise counsel. Dr. Matt Carrano of the Smithsonian has also offered percep-tive comments. At Hylas, editor Marcel Brousseau has been a pleasure to work with, and Aaron Murray has oiled the wheels well. And I am indebted, as ever, to my wife Jane for her unstinting support.

Leslie Mertz: This book is for every parent, grand-parent, aunt, and uncle who ever bought a set of toy dinosaurs for a little boy or girl; and for the paleontologists who have never gotten over their childhood dinosaur days.

The authors and publisher also offer thanks to those closely involved in the creation of this volume: Dr. Matthew Carrano, of the National Museum of Natural History; consultant Dr. Jason J. Head, of the University of Toronto; copyeditor Carole Campbell; editor Christina Wiginton of Smithsonian Books; Smithsonian photographer Chip Clark; Collins Reference executive editor Donna Sanzone, editor Lisa Hacken, and editorial assistant Stephanie Mey-ers; Hydra Publishing president Sean Moore, publish-ing director Karen Prince, editorial director Aaron Murray, art director Brian MacMullen, editor Amber Rose, editor Marcel Brousseau, designers Eunho Lee and Erika Lubowicki, picture researcher Ben DeWalt, senior editor Lisa Purcell, editors Suzanne Lander, Andy Lawler, Rachael Lanicci, Ward Calhoun, and Sylke Jackson. Also, many thanks to Gabriel Lio, and John and Bridgette Sibbick.

CREDITS

The following abbreviations are used: JI—© 2007 Jupiterimages Corporation; PR—Photo Researchers, Inc.; ISP—© iStockPhoto.com; SS—ShutterStock; IO—Index Open; BS—Big Stock Photo; BMP—© BMPhoto; Wi—Wikimedia; LOC—Library of Congress; NPS—National Park Service

(t=top; b=bottom; l=left; r=right; c=center)

Monsters of the Mesozoic
iii BMP and JI iv–v Michael Rissi/Wi vi © John Sibbick 2 Photo Adventures, LLC/ISP 2 John Fergusson Cathcart/Wi 3 Chip Clark/SI 4 © John Sibbick 5 Laurie O'Keefe/PR 6 NASA 7 © Ron Blakey 7 © Ron Blakey 7 © Ron Blakey 8–9 Jozef Sedmak/SS 10–11 Mario Tarello/SS

Chapter 1: Biggest Meat-Eaters
12–13 © John Sibbick 14 © John Sibbick 16 Samuel Griswold Goodrich 17 Wi 18 BMP 19 © John Sibbick 20 Scott Sanders/SS 22 © John Sibbick 25 Denis Paquin/AP 26 Adrian Chesterman/ISP 27 Steveoc 86/Wi

Chapter 2: Biggest Plant-Eaters
28 BMP 30 Luna04/Wi 31 Christian Darkin/SS 32-33 Joe Tucciarone/PR 34 Gabriel Lio/Museo Argentino de Ciencias Naturales 36 Laurie Minor-Penland/SI 37 © John Sibbick 39 © John Sibbick 40 © John Sibbick

Chapter 3: Small and Dainty
42 © John Sibbick 43 Ballista/Wi 44 Mario Tarello/SS 45 Scott Feldstein/Wi 46 Mariana Ruiz/Wi 48 BMP 50 Mario Tarello/SS 51 Matt Martyniuk/Wi

Chapter 4: Anatomical Extremes
52 © John Sibbick 54 Raimond Spekking/Wi 55 JI 57 © John Sibbick 58 Joe Ashley 59 Arthur Weasley/Wi 60 Roger Harris/PR 61 Ballista/Wi 62 BMP 63 © John Sibbick 64 Arthur Weasley/Wi 65 Mario Tarello/SS 66 Ballista/Wi 67 Bob Ainsworth/SS 68 © John Sibbick 69 JI 70 Johan Swanepoel/SS 71 © John Sibbick

Chapter 5: First and Last
72 © John Sibbick 74 Lynsey Allan/SS 75 Ismael Montero Verdu/SS 76 © John Sibbick 77 Wi 78 cosmopol/ISP 79 © John Sibbick 80 Laurie O'Keefe/PR 81 jynus/Wi 82 Ismael Montero Verdu/SS 83 © John Sibbick 84 Ballista/Firsfron/Wi 85 Chip Clark/Smithsonian Institution 86 Christoph Ermel/ISP 87 Chip Clark/SI

Chapter 6: Extremely Extinct
88 © John Sibbick 90 DanielCD/Wi 91 Glenlarson/Wi 92 Charlie Borland/IO 93 USGS 94 Courtesy NASA/JPL-Caltech 95 Courtesy NASA/JPL-Caltech 96 Mark Garlick/PR

Chapter 7: On the Prowl
98–99 © John Sibbick 100 © John Sibbick 102 Francois Gohier/PR 103 Daderot/Wi 104 BMP 105 BMP 106 JI 108 John Rodriguez/ISP 109 © John Sibbick 110 Nick Biemans/SS 111 Joe Ashley

Chapter 8: The Vegetarian Option
112 Christian Darkin/PR 114 Ballista/Wi 116 BMP 117 BMP 118tr BMP 118bl christiandarkin/ISP 119 BMP 120 BMP 121 BMP

Chapter 9: Self-Defense
122 © John Sibbick 124 Mariana Ruiz/Wi 126 Ballista/Wi 127 Mariana Ruiz Villarreal/Wi 128 BMP 129 BMP 130 Joe Tucciarone/PR 131 © John Sibbick 132 Mark Garlick/PR 133 BMP

Chapter 10: Survival Tactics
134–35 © John Sibbick 136 © John Sibbick 138 Laurie O'Keefe/PR 139 Mark Hammon/ISP 140 Marcio Luiz/Wi 141 Francois Gohier/PR 142 Dave Housekhecht/USGS 143 © John Sibbick

Chapter 11: The Trials of Breeding
144 © John Sibbick 146 Laurie Minor-Penland/SI 147 Steveoc 86/Wi 148 BMP 149 Sam Lee/ISP 150 BMP 151 BMP

Chapter 12: Early Rivalry
152–53 © John Sibbick 154 Michael Overton/Wi 156 Wi 157 Wi 158 Ballista/Wi 159 Wi 160 Wi 161 Wi 162 Wi 163 Wi 164 LadyofArts/Wi 165 LadyofArts/Wi 166tl Wi 166br Ballista/Wi 167 Keith Schengili-Roberts/Wi 168 Wi 168 Wi 169 Wi 170tl © John Sibbick 170b Szabolcs Borbely/SS 171 Wi

Chapter 13: Difficult and Dangerous Work
172 Medvedev Vladmir/SS 174tr BMP 174bl Mario Tarello/SS 175tr V. J. Matthew/SS 175bl Wi 176tr Richard Goerg/ISP 176bl Mario Tarello/SS 177 Joe Ashley 178tr Raimond Spekking/Wi 178br Wi 179 Mario Tarello/SS 180 LOC 181tr Mario Tarello/SS 181b Louise Shumbris/SS 182t Cora Reed/SS 182b Wi 183 © John Sibbick 184 BMP 185tr LadyofHats/Wi 185tl BMP 186 Mario Tarello/SS 187tr Wi 187br Wi

Chapter 14: More and More Extreme
188 © John Sibbick 190 Mario Tarello/SS 191 Carlos Goldin/Photo Researchers 192tc Debivort/WI 192b Mario Tarello/SS 193tr LadyOfHats/Wi 193br LadyOfHats/Wi 194bl © John Sibbick 195tr Laikayiu/Wi 195br Laikayiu/Wi 196 J. Nguyen/Wi 197 Wi 198tr Bryngelzon/ISP 198bl B. W. Hamilton/NPS 199 Duard van der Westhuizen/ISP 200 Richard T. Nowitz /PR

At the Smithsonian
208 Vladimir Ivanov/ISP 209 Dane A. Penland/SI 210tl Dane A. Penland/SI 210br Laurie Minor-Penland/SI 211tl Laurie Minor-Penland/SI 211r Scott Sampson/SI

Cover Art
Front BMP and JI **Back** Mike Grindley/SS

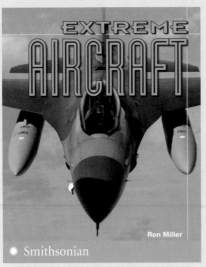
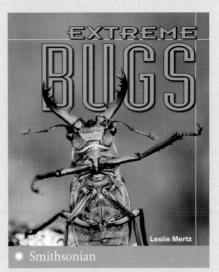
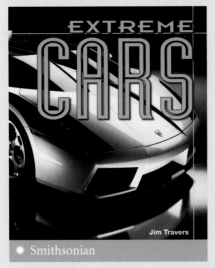
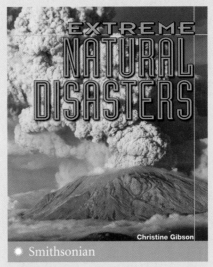
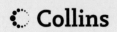
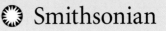